THE

Intuitive Leadership
Inspiring a New Dream of Earth

Patti O'Donahue, M.A.

BALBOA.
PRESS

A DIVISION OF HAY HOUSE

Balboa Press books may be ordered through booksellers or by contacting:

Balboa Press
A Division of Hay House
1663 Liberty Drive
Bloomington, IN 47403
www.balboapress.com
1 (877) 407-4847

Because of the dynamic nature of the Internet, any web addresses or links contained in this book may have changed since publication and may no longer be valid. The views expressed in this work are solely those of the author and do not necessarily reflect the views of the publisher, and the publisher hereby disclaims any responsibility for them.

The author of this book does not dispense medical advice or prescribe the use of any technique as a form of treatment for physical, emotional, or medical problems without the advice of a physician, either directly or indirectly. The intent of the author is only to offer information of a general nature to help you in your quest for emotional and spiritual well-being. In the event you use any of the information in this book for yourself, which is your constitutional right, the author and the publisher assume no responsibility for your actions.

Any people depicted in stock imagery provided by Thinkstock are models, and such images are being used for illustrative purposes only.
Certain stock imagery © Thinkstock.

Printed in the United States of America.

ISBN: 978-1-4525-8443-0 (sc)
ISBN: 978-1-4525-8444-7 (e)

Balboa Press rev. date: 11/19/2013

Table of Contents

All My Relations

Dedication

These words are dedicated to my daughter, Sascha, who as a little girl re-awakened me to the mysterious nature of the universe and to our gift of intuition; a divine source of knowing. I also devote the following pages to her son and my grandson, Nixon Euchere. This sweet little boy, although only five years old at the time of this writing has been another profound teacher in my unlearning and remembering about other ways of knowing. Just like his Mama, Nixon is in tune with a greater mystery and communicates this wisdom to the adults around that are open and willing to listen.

I dedicate this conversation to my Elders and Ancestors; as well as to the First Nation's peoples whom I have had the honor of working with over this past decade. Despite generations of trauma indigenous peoples have remained connected to their heart, and to the heartbeat of Mother Earth and the Great Spirit. Indigenous peoples have a unique worldview and are teachers in the unfolding of a New Dream of Earth.

We are living through a global paradigm shift, a transformational time in human consciousness when antiquated beliefs that no longer serve life are falling away and new beliefs, values and perceptions are arising. We are at the crossroads with many complex problems to overcome. Problems that require new ways of seeing, being and doing and intuitive intelligence is a jewel residing within the heart of all available for inspiration and guidance.

Lastly, I honour these chapters to the rise of the feminine within the world and to the peaceful integration of all cultures and creatures onto a single planet. Imagining a future where our children, grandchildren and great grandchildren have a healthy harmonious home, community and earth to live out their wildest dreams.

Namaste

The Gift

The Intuitive mind
Is a sacred Gift
And the rational mind
Is a faithful servant
We have created a society
That honors the servant
And has forgotten the Gift

Albert Einstein

The Gift

Forward

   As little children, most of us explore the world around us with delightful curiosity. Over time though, the experiences we gather along the way solidify to form our beliefs and our perceptions regarding the nature of reality. The majority of western society is logically based and factually grounded in the day to day activities of living, while others walk on this earth as travelers of consciousness and the invisible realms of dreams, insights and intuitions.

   It is the world of dreams, insights and intuitions that we will journey into. *A way of knowing without knowing how we know what we know.*

   The idea that we are connected to a Great Mystery is a way of being still embodied by indigenous cultures, little children, scientists, artists and healers. Every moment, every wish and every challenge is yet another opportunity to engage in a magical and invisible process that Einstein referred to as the *"The Gift."* The gift is the miracle of intuitive insight that has the capacity to open our hearts and minds to new dimensions of reality while deepening our subtle relationship to our Self and our world.

   Our global family is rich in diverse expressions of reality providing a multicolored lens that shines crystalline light into unique ways of seeing, knowing and being in the world.

Knowledge sharing through technology, the internet and globalization is removing some of the previous stigma attached to human diversity and opening up our awareness to the gifts of perceptual differences.

The restricting beliefs of the past that kept human beings neatly boxed are slowly dissolving, allowing individuals from all walks, ages and cultures to more openly share their lens, experience and learnings. An example of this is a young man born color blind who can, with the aid of technology, listen to the sound of color as felt in his bones. His name, is Neil Harbisson and he has also learned to create music from the frequencies he senses emanating from physical objects. Frequencies that he then translates into notes or colors that become songs or paintings. This young man is challenging our idea of what is possible and transforming a perceived disability into a unique lens of reality.

Dr. Jill Bolte Taylor, a Harvard trained neuroanatomist who suffered a debilitating stroke that damaged the left hemisphere of her brain is yet another example of changing perceptions. Dr. Bolte Taylor used her knowledge of science to explore and learn from her health condition and she is changing the way we think. The two hemispheres of our brain are known to have very different functions. The left brain being linear, logical and methodical with the capacity to process and file enormous amounts of detail documenting our past experiences and projecting it into our future reality. This region of the brain also gives us our sense of "I Am" a perception that provides human beings with their sense of separateness from life and from each other. The left brain defines our body as a separate entity that is disconnected from the energy fields that surround us. A reality that dominates society today, as is evident in most social structures and relationships.

The stroke that Dr. Bolte Taylor experienced opened her up to a whole new world of consciousness. According to her, this was a world of bliss where the energy of all life is interconnected to the individual and is a reality experienced by mystics, shamans and wisdom teachers. A state of consciousness where all boundaries cease to exist and are replaced with a magnificent sense of oneness. A place where profound states of joy and bliss are considered normal. In this state of being we become more conscious of our own energy and the energy of those surrounding us, aware of the various different frequencies being transmitted and received. Through this sense, our life becomes more compassionate, more peaceful, and begins to vibrate with exquisite beauty.

The place where all life becomes one through our interconnectedness is the place where intuitive knowing can be found. Indigenous peoples call this the web of life and when we surrender to this vibratory web we can know that which was previously unknowable. The genius Albert Einstein embraced his capacity for intuitive insight openly giving credit for his ability to solve complex problems to this mysterious source of wisdom. An ability for individuals to become a channel for divine knowledge, an intelligence beyond intellect and reason.

Research indicates that most genius's embrace their intuition as a valid way of knowing. Like the fairy tale of old about the genie in the bottle, once released from the confines of conditioned thinking individuals have access to a vast resource. The ability to frame a question and then wait patiently for intuitive insight is never seen by a genius as flaky, weird or crazy. It is a completely natural way of knowing.

Intuition is a highly valued and respected gift given to all those who seek answers with the confident belief that the universe will provide in its own time and in its own way. We may not understand the magic afoot, but we can learn to appreciate the gift of intuition through our conscious connection with a divine source of wisdom. A source of wisdom that communicates to each of us and is available for inspiration and problem solving on the individual and collective level. It is our own personal GPS, Guru and Genie; providing insight while guiding us along to higher levels of understanding and awareness.

I was born into a family of intuitives and blessed to have two wise women with these gifts situated on both sides of my family tree. These women were from very different backgrounds but were similar in that they both were sought after for their wisdom, insight and healing nature. My earliest memories as a little girl were also intuitive or having a sense of being connected to a vast source of knowledge that was beyond myself.

The result of growing up in a family where dreams that saw into the future and voices that spoke that were not your own led to my becoming comfortable with the idea that other realities existed beyond what was considered normal. As I got older though, I went through a shift away from my intuitive source. Slowly and unconsciously I adopted the beliefs of the dominant society and over time effectively disconnected myself from this source of knowing.

The process of reconnecting to this sixth sense began when my daughter was born as it was obvious that she was connected to a source beyond that of normal adult awareness. My reconnection was strengthened once again with the birth of my grandson as he also had the gift of telepathy and intuitive knowing. These little people demonstrated an ability to simply know from a place of total innocence similar to the main character in the movie, "The Green Mile" who often knows without ever having been told. When asked how he knows, he responds that he does not know and that he has never known (intellectually) much.

My childhood experiences left me curious and with many unanswered questions. Researching the realms of intuition and the invisible world, along with its potential for leadership within individuals and the collective human family became a personal quest.

What is this source of knowledge? Why are we not cultivating intuitive wisdom within our children, and our families and organizations? If a genius respects their intuition and understands how to access it to solve complex problems, why aren't we teaching it in our schools and learning institutions? Why is there so much suffering on Earth? Why is society fearful of alternative ways of knowing? Why are intuitive individuals so often ridiculed and called "crazy?" How can the stigma be removed from intuition to create a respectful platform for other ways of knowing to be openly explored and shared?

The desire to share intuitive stories was heightened after a vision I received in 2010 while on a yoga retreat in Baja, Mexico marking my fiftieth birthday.

The Vision

The Vision

I am diving down and further down, deep into the dark depths of the ocean and sense that I am being gently guided on a journey by an ancient feminine presence. I intuit this guiding presence as the energy of the Grandmothers and in a few gliding strokes I am swimming alongside a pod of majestic whales, whom I understand represent the Grandmothers of the sea. The single eye of an old female looks directly into mine and with a wisdom that transcends time she begins to telepathically communicate information through sonar and sight. Images of the past, present and future are rapidly transferred through our visual connection as generations of her species experiences in the waters of time rapidly flip by as if on a film in my consciousness.

"It is time," she gently says. It is time for human beings to return to the homeland within their own heart and begin speaking their truth. She further communicates that the ability of the ocean's creatures is reaching the limits of its capacity. The pollution, the unnatural and dissonant frequencies, the disease and the environmental stressors caused by human activity are causing illness and massive die offs in the sea. This message is repeated in various forms time and time again as a rapid succession of the oceans diverse creatures rapidly appear, adding their silent voice and then vanishing quickly into the darkness of the ocean. They all communicate the same simple, but powerful message. **"It is time!"**

In a flash, I am transported back up through the depths of the ocean and find myself up upon the surface of a dusty and barren landscape. In spirit form I am now gliding alongside a large herd of elephants who one by one take turns gazing into my soul. The ancient female presence informs me that the elephants are the Grandmothers of the Earth.

After a time, a single wizened old female takes the lead plodding alongside me and once again through the transmission sent from a single right eye she communicates her message along with the emotion of great sadness. The ancient female elephant shares that her species is growing ever more tired of the needless destruction on the planet and is concerned about the future if patterns do not change and soon. The Grandmother Elephant shares the same story as the Grandmother Whale. *"It is time for human beings to return home to the truth within their own hearts and collectively begin speaking from their authentic voice."* I continue gliding along beside the elephants while a rapid succession of land creatures, collectively rich in diversity and beauty whirl past me communicating through non-verbal language a similar message. **It is time to return to the home in our hearts and speak our authentic voice of truth.**

At a certain point in time I am guided to leave the barren dry landscape and in a single quick sweep I am soaring high up into the blue sky. Once again in the form of Spirit I am able to transform states simply by thought. The birds of flight are traveling in large flocks and surround me in every direction that I can see. Flocks of brightly colored birds fly by me while communicating the now shared vision of transformation. The need for radical changes in human consciousness and in patterns of behavior regarding our relationship to ourselves, our nations, the earth and all life.

"**It is time!**" the various flocks sing while we glide in synchronicity, making delightful swooping and swirling designs throughout the sky as we circle the planet. I he creatures of the sky, are also stressed, sick and dying from the mounting air pollution and the steady bombardment of frequencies that disorientate their natural guiding systems with Mother Earth and to each other. The winged ones communicate that human beings must return home to their hearts. To the place of feeling where we can listen deeply to our song and find the courage to sing that song of individual truth broadcasting our voices to the world as the destructive patterns of humanity need to stop, and very soon . . .

The Grandmothers of the elements of water, land and air had spoken.

Returning Home

I find myself awakening into another state of consciousness. Slowly, I become aware of my physical body and realize that I am lying on the floor in a yoga studio close to a beach. I am returning home, and can hear my heart beating and the pounding ocean waves. I feel a loving young presence beside me that I remember as Jackie who gently supports me as I become increasingly more conscious of my body and my physical surroundings.

It is just past my fiftieth birthday and as a rite of passage I have taken yoga teacher training in Baja, Mexico. I am the Elder within this group of over fifteen beautiful young women and a single brave male, all of whom are radiant with glowing health. I embarked upon this journey of yoga, dance and meditation to clear my mind, challenge my body and awaken my spirit as I make the transition into this later stage of my life. Sluggishly all of the floor bound yogi's rise up and come together in a circle to share their stories. We have just participated in a form of pranayama or transformative breath work designed to connect us back to the home within our own soul to listen and to learn from our inner wisdom. I am the only Grandmother in the group and as a result my personal experience may reflect my age and role in this stage of life.

The process of becoming a Grandmother is a transcendental journey into a unique perception of reality. A portal into timelessness that weaves past, present and future generations together into a single strand. The passage of becoming a Grandmother heightened my awareness of my own limiting beliefs, blocks and repeating patterns; encouraging ongoing reflection, integration and transformation.

The vision I received from the Grandmothers was a call to courageous action. A nudging to continue striving towards greater forms of wholeness by expressing the truth that is only mine, and towards the reality where *"I Am"* living within in the Great Mystery where *"All is One."* However, the ancient feminine presence was a calling for more than just my own truth and authenticity though. It was a call to use my life experience and knowledge to encourage the awakening of authenticity and truth in others. This is my response.

We live in a time on Mother Earth that is overflowing with complex systemic challenges, most caused by human activity. Many people believe that we are at the crossroads and need to evolve into higher states of consciousness as the path we are on is not sustainable. We appear to have become desensitized to suffering and somehow disconnected from our natural feeling state, our true nature. The main character in the movie "Powder" is highly sensitive to electromagnetic energy, he is psychic, compassionate and understanding to all beings with a depth of knowing that most humans do not have. He is considered a genius and for all these gifts he is ridiculed, ostracized and beat up. Powder shares his insight during a conversation with a girlfriend where he explains that human beings see themselves as separate, and that sense of separation affects our ability to feel, to know and to truly understand the natural world. I agree with this statement.

In terms of leadership we are in a period of transition when old ways of being and doing are falling away as they do not support life as we know it today. The bridging between two worldviews is full of opportunities to explore new ideas and to apply new ways of thinking. Intuitive leadership is a fusion of ideas into one such model, amongst many, for the new earth we are birthing. Innovation, creativity and intuitive insight are forms of divine wisdom that can be nurtured within individuals, children, families and organizations. All that is required is an open heart and mind, stillness and time to connect and listen to our inner voice.

We are born into this world with a joyous sense of divine connection, or intuition, which far too often gets lost as we grow into adulthood. Returning home is the restoration of that childlike sense of wonder and innocent wisdom where our intuitive self can be found.

Humanity is Part of the Whole Universe

A human being is a part of the whole, called by us the "Universe."

He experiences his thoughts and feelings as something separated from the rest, a kind of optical delusion of his consciousness.

This delusion is a kind of prison for us, restricting us to our personal desires and to affection for a few persons nearest to us.

Our task must be to free ourselves from this prison by widening our circle of compassion to embrace all living creatures and the whole of nature in its beauty."

Albert Einstein

Living in the Mystery

Do You Know Who You Are?

"Do you know who you are?" The shaman asked.

A thick silence filled the short distance between us.

"Do you know who you are?" she repeated, her eyes locking mine so forcefully she might as well have put her hands on either side of my face. Responses were racing through me like the reels of a slot machine. But I remained silent as huge tears started to slide down my cheeks.

I knew who I was, but I had no idea how to express it. I didn't know how to mirror on the outside the truth of who I was within.

I had come to the shaman because I ardently believed she could flip a switch and change me. I believed that I would meet something or someone outside of myself— the right word, a wise thought, a sacred text, a spiritual master—that would touch my soul, and that would be it. Boom! I would be aligned with the truth of who I am. I would again be connected to that sense of love and freedom that I knew without question as a little girl.

Meggan Watterson

The Story of a Little Girl

I was fortunate enough to spend the majority of my childhood playing in the natural wonders of this world. Openly soaking up Mother Nature's brilliant colors and diverse beauty while riding my pony through the fields, swimming in the ocean or meandering along the trails in the forest. My family lived on several farms, and in this peaceful place of tranquility I was often struck by a profound sense of awesomeness. A joyful feeling of grand interconnectedness with all of life. I embodied this fairy like sense of "being" as if a mystical creature wondering through a magical land. I knew without a doubt that I belonged to the earth and the stars.

As a little girl, I also learned to listen to the language spoken deep within the silence of my own Soul. I could hear the wisdom of Mother Nature's knowing ways if I tuned in and listened to her voice. In my later years, I discovered that this sensitivity led me to perceive the world through a lens similar to that of a mystic, shaman or indigenous peoples. This was the world I inhabited and a world that perhaps most children exist in. A place of profound connection with the land, the water and the air where all dimensions were alive and pulsating with vibrating energy. I was in continuous communication with everything in existence and I was free to be me.

Indigenous peoples and wisdom traditions refer to this feeling of interconnectedness as the web of life. In scientific terms the web of life may also be known as a field, the matrix or a living system. The field, living system, matrix or web of life is like a sea of information that surrounds us at all times and like the spider sitting at the center of her web, a sensitive person can feel and interpret the subtle vibrations emanating everywhere. In indigenous cultures the spider is known as the communicator, and like the spider from Charlotte's Web sensitive's can understand the language of the both worlds, the internal and the external.

A Hindu philosopher once taught his disciple that the world is not only made by God, but made of God as well. "How can that be?" inquired the pupil. "Look at the spider" replied the teacher, "who with the utmost intelligence draws the threads of its wonderful net out of its own body." The God of the Hindus is sometimes perceived as a large spider sitting in the center of the Universe and believe there are invisible thread like structures interconnecting everything. If you look at the brilliant art work of Norval Morriseau, a shaman artist from Canada who paints in bright and beautiful colors and a closer zoom in reveals tiny strings connecting all of the physical objects in his paintings.

As mentioned, I am blessed to come from a family tree with intuitives on both sides, and was fortunate enough to grow up listening to stories about dreams, insights and voices that spoke from within that were not your own, and of knowing without knowing how you knew. In my worldview, intuition was a curious gift that we were given and not a sign of our insanity. You just simply know and accept that you do not know the source of this knowing. Our family never attended church, nor did we speak openly about God or religion. There was however, a shared understanding that a mysterious intelligence existed beyond the individual self and that this intelligence could be trusted upon for wise counsel.

As a child and young adult I could travel to other places in my dreams and had an intuitive sense about people. I was deeply in tune with my spirit and although tiny in stature I had a warrior like strength that challenged my parents. My mother was a gentle soul and preferred that I told lies and learned to pretend and keep the peace.

Like all children though I often said things that my parents would have preferred I didn't. Telling the truth felt essential to my nature and at times this truth was at odds with my childhood reality. My father was an alcoholic and prone to taking out his rage on his wife or his children, but for the most part he left me alone. His disrespect towards the people I loved enraged me and I refused to remain silent.

As mentioned, we lived on beautiful farms with gorgeous pastures for the horses and cows, lush west coast forests and streams, ponds and wetlands. The natural world of my childhood was heaven to my heart and a haven from the dysfunctional home environment I found myself living within. It was here in the natural world that I found my strength and protection. I believed that fairies and spirits inhabited the landscape and that they supported me as I walked in this world. While frolicking in Mother Nature I never felt any sense of aloneness, even if I was. Every day was an adventure where my entire being could drink in the surrounding beauty. I had rocks to climb, ponds and streams to wade in and animals to talk to. In the barnyard, we had up to ten horses, at one time sixty calves, a milk cow, two pigs and a chicken coop with twenty clucking hens for fresh eggs, along with three dogs and countless cats. This was my world and I truly loved being in it.

In the sixties and seventies, driving into the city was a painful experience because I would lose my normal sense of felt self. I found the vehicle exhaust painful to inhale which led me to cover my nose with a piece of fabric. The pavement, the noise and the buildings broke my energetic connection with the web of life and left me feeling uncomfortable in my body and to survive I needed to shut down.

Everywhere I looked I saw this grey landscape instead of the lush country green scape full of rich textures and visual stimulation. In the city my eyes saw only starlings and crows instead of a rich diversity of insects and songbirds, blue birds, eagles and herons. In my heart this grey empty landscape translated into a great sadness in my heart and I couldn't wait to get back home to the peace of nature where I could open up again.

I am so glad that so many conscious people have worked diligently to transform our cities into sustainable living communities where human beings can once again be in touch with nature and wild creatures have a place to call home. It is wonderful that many of our modern cities are thriving with activity and people are enjoying the outdoors by walking, jogging, cycling, and chatting in sidewalk cafes or viewing the arts and entertainment integrated into the streetscape. A glorious transformation of urban space bringing comfort to sensitive people like myself.

It was this sensitivity and interconnectedness that I took with me into the bigger world of social systems and that further shaped my perception of reality.

A Young Woman

The Forming of Beliefs

In high school, while taking a Grade 9 math class I discovered that I could solve complex algebra or word problems without having a clue how I arrived at the answer. Not all of the time, but enough to be noticeable. When called upon by the teacher to explain to the class my problem solving process all I could do was look at him with utter confusion, shrug my shoulders and blush. I had no idea. Was it important? My technique seemed random and illogical, and I could not explain my process through the structured steps as instructed by the teacher. I found this ability extremely embarrassing and eventually concluded that I must not be very intelligent. To avoid any further embarrassment I dropped out of math completely, and transferred from the academic program to a class of students with known learning and behavioral difficulties. Although these young people were considered "troublesome" I thrived in this environment as I was able to learn art, poetry and language, and I resonated with the rebellion, mischievousness and laughter so often present in the classroom.

Dissolving Beliefs

Despite my difficulties with math in high school I loved learning and in my thirties I decided to challenge my high school beliefs by returning to school as an adult learner. To start with though, I had to upgrade my math beginning back where I left off in Grade 9. Although fearful, I managed to overcome my blocks and learn the sequential steps to logical problem-solving. Much to my surprise and without intention I found myself entering graduate school for leadership and training in my early forties.

The Master's program required learners to take several personality and learning assessments to increase self-awareness and self-knowledge, which are key to effective leadership. One of the assessments was Myers Briggs or MBTI originally developed by Carl Jung where I learned that I was an INFP which translated into Introverted (although on the cusp with Extroverted) Intuitive, Feeling and Perceptive. According to the Myers Briggs assessment, these were my learning style preferences. This was an epiphany or "Aha" moment as the results provided insight into my learning style and all my challenges in high school became clear.

With this new information my entire sense of self shifted radically. Reference materials stated that individuals with an intuitive preference are known to have an ability to solve math problems without using a logical sequential process to arrive at an answer. This was not a learning dis-ability as I had thought. ***It was a gift!*** I discovered that I was a visionary or big picture person and tended to start at the end working my way backwards in a random and illogical fashion. Therefore, I found linear thinking and attention to small details exhausting as it required using the less dominant areas of my brain. The left side verses the right side of my brain.

What I learned in graduate school opened up my life forever. This single realization provided me with a much needed explanation for my ability to know the answers to complex problems without understanding the process. My beliefs could now be reframed into a new and more positive sense of self rooted in an understanding of both my strengths and my weaknesses. I wish that all teachers and students were taught about people with intuitive ways of knowing. A way of knowing that must be honored and somehow integrated into the curriculum of educational systems to bring about a greater acceptance and understanding of the gifts of human diversity.

*To remember who you are you need to forget
who they told you to be.*

Travel & Unlearning

After completing high school, I thirsted for adventure and began to backpack to various parts of the world where I learned more about the intuitive process. My travel experiences taught me to trust that I would meet the right people at the right time and that I would be guided to a place to stay, a place to eat or a person who would take me on a journey that would open up my perception of reality.

In 1979, at the age of eighteen I flew down to Mexico with a friend as we planned to travel across the country. We touched down in Cancun first and after being hit with torrential rains that flooded the streets we jumped on a small boat and headed out to Isle Mujeres, or *"Island of the Women."* I loved this beautiful oasis where my friend and I met wonderful fellow travelers, danced all night on white sand beaches, snorkeled with tropical fish, slept in hammocks and rented motorbikes to tour the island. It was on this island that I saw my first ancient ruin and although it was fairly insignificant by comparison to other Mayan sites there was something about just being in the place that triggered subtle memories and touched me deeply.

With great sadness, we departed Isle Mujeres on a small ferry and then climbed aboard a rickety bus to Chichen Itza, deep in the heart of the Yucatan. Today Chichen Itza is a World Heritage Site and was recently designated one of the Seven

Wonders of the World and as a world renowned destination it is packed with tourists every day of the year. But back in 1979, over 30 years ago, only a few hard core tourists and archaeologists made the journey. After a hot, bumpy and stimulating ride, we arrived at our destination and stepped off the bus in the middle of what seemed like nowhere.

Chichen Itza is located in the small village of Piste and is on route to the larger historical city of Merida. After a short walk on dirt roads we located a hotel and booked a room for a few nights. I still have a postcard from this place which has an image of a beautiful five star hotel. But in reality the hotel was never finished and our glass patio doors looked out upon a swimming pool half filled with green slimy water and above the first floor were various levels of unfinished walls complete with rusty rebar spikes poking out in all directions. The gap between the postcard image and the reality was humorous and I hope that the vision has been fulfilled for tourists today.

After settling in and asking for directions we headed out on foot down the dusty dirt road towards Chichen Itza, the famous ancient Mayan ruin. The site was surrounded by a barbed wire fence and besides a few meandering cows and people we pretty much had the ruins to explore for ourselves. The landscape was breathtaking and I was completely mesmerized by the magnificence of the site. The stone construction was unimaginable and challenged everything my mind knew with regards to human history and knowledge. There was this sense of timeless intelligence infused within every stone that was mysterious; leaving me bewildered and confused.

I had just finished school and yet I had no memory of learning anything about these people. My studies were primarily focused on the ancient peoples of Europe and the Middle East. Why? This civilization was obviously advanced in astronomy, mathematics, the arts and architecture and should have had a higher profile in my studies regarding human history.

The stone structures included what I believed was a healing sanctuary, an observatory, the largest known ball court in the Americas, a road system, advanced stone work and construction. The most prominent stone structure was the Temple of Kukulkan, or El Castillo, a pyramid that demonstrated the accuracy of the Mayan astronomy having a total of 365 steps, divided between the four sides and the top plateau. Twice a year on the spring and autumn equinoxes the shadow of a serpent appears and winds its way down the steps to join the stone serpent head at the base of the pyramid. How could an ancient civilization with primitive knowledge demonstrate such accuracy in designing timeless structures in alignment with the heavens?

With the passing of December 21st, 2012 awareness of the Mayan Calendar and it's calculation of the beginnings and endings of nine cycles spread throughout the world, but in 1979 I knew nothing of this. The Mayan Calendar is a story about the cosmic energies that impact the earth, humanity and the universe leading to evolutions in consciousness. The first cycle goes all the way back to 16 billion years ago with the forming of galaxies and arrives all the way up to the modern era. According to the Mayans, during this era humanity will release former destructive belief systems shifting into a new cycle that will be based upon equality, respect for nature and unity consciousness.

As mentioned though, I was unaware of any of this information on the Mayan people or their calendar. But I was very aware on another level. As I wandered throughout the ruins I felt like I had stepped through a veil separating two distinct worlds, the world of the Mayan peoples and my own. There was a spiritual presence that resonated within the landscape prompting deep questioning of my own personal truths regarding the nature of reality.

On one particular day, shortly before dusk I climbed atop the Temple of Warriors, a smaller pyramid directly across from the Temple of Kukulkan. I am afraid of heights and this smaller structure was a more manageable climb than the steep steps of Kukulkan which was too high for consideration. Upon reaching the stone plateau, I sat in quiet meditative stillness taking in the magnificence of the ancient site and waiting for any intuitive insight to arise. I did not have to wait long before a voice from deep within me said with strength and conviction, *"Nothing you have learned is true."*

There was a confident clarity to the voice within letting me know that it my intuitive intelligence communicating. The message was a puzzle though as I had just completed twelve years of school, and although I had my math challenges I knew that I loved learning. Also, at the time I could not conceive of a reality where my parents and society would have me dedicate that length of time to anything if it wasn't important and valuable. My days of wandering throughout the ancient Mayan civilization had opened a floodgate of questions regarding the truth about human history.

It was only much later, and after years and years of higher learning that I arrived at a place of being so disillusioned by the educational system that I dropped out of university in my third year. I dropped out because I felt the educational system wanted to reward students for their ability to memorize outdated information that repeated dysfunctional antiquated systems and behaviors instead of nurturing learners to question and discover truth for themselves. The learning process of academia felt robotic and lacked the space for individual thought and ideas.

As a mature student, I knew that far too much of the information I was learning was in actual fact the very reason our planet was being destroyed and that millions of people were suffering. The educational system was dominated by linear thinking, exploitation of planetary resources and the use of vulnerable people for profit. My heart longed to hear what a woman in history felt or a how a female leader thought. To jump into higher learning with such enthusiasm only to have male ideas, egos and knowledge transmitted through texts and professors regarding the nature of truth and reality was insulting to my feminine intelligence. Without the integration of the feminine worldview into all disciplines our world was visibly out of balance and teetering on the edge of destruction, and I was angry.

As a woman dedicated to holistic thinking and human and ecological transformation the higher learning I so eagerly sought and paid for was promoting all of the very beliefs I had spent my life working to change. These beliefs were based upon separateness and not interconnectedness; of economic development and insatiable greed instead of sustainable development; of linear thinking verses holistic creative thinking; of silent obedience and memorization of antiquated beliefs instead of critical analysis and self-determination. Of truth and knowledge from a perspective dominated by a male worldview instead of inclusive of the wisdom of women, minorities and children. I dropped out disillusioned with the educational system and not knowing what to do with my life. I could not ethically continue to invest my time and money learning information that did not serve me or the healing of the Mother Earth, whom I saw as a living being.

In 2002, I learned about the Master of Arts Degree in Leadership and Training at Royal Roads University in Victoria, BC. The research I conducted indicated that this could be a cutting edge learning environment open to the diverse knowledge of the learners. Furthermore, it was my understanding that ideas could be openly debated allowing adult learners to establish truth according to their own values and perception of reality. It appeared that this could be the learning environment I had long searched for and a place where I could study the transformative leadership styles that I had been drawn to throughout my life. These included visionary and spiritual leaders such as: Gandhi, Nelson Mandela, Rabindranath Tagore, Sitting Bull, The Dalai Lama, Norval Morrisseau, Chief Dan George, Black Elk, Martin Luther King and many other wisdom teachers of our times.

These visionaries embodied a sense of interconnectedness with all of life and transformed the world through their ability to peacefully communicate a holy vision, forever transforming the world through the power of peace, creativity and love. Although there is an obvious lack of female representation in my list of leaders, these men were integrated in both the feminine and masculine, and therefore, able to speak to a woman's heart and mind. This is our language.

It was much further down my path before I could begin to grasp the history driving the loss of the feminine voice in leadership, knowledge making and social structures in so many nations throughout the planet.

Guides Back into the Mystery

Our Children & Grandchildren

My Daughter

In my early twenties I gave birth to my beautiful baby girl, Sascha Rose. Even as a little baby she had star like qualities, not like those of a movie star but this inner glow and radiance. Her heart was pure and she embodied love and a gentle kindness, perpetually bubbling over with joy and happiness. A light shone from deep within her chocolate brown eyes that sparked a remembering of something that I once knew; but had long since forgotten.

Around the age of two while driving in the car, I playfully asked her, "Where did you come from anyway?" She immediately pointed out the window and up to the sky and said with delight, "I came from the sky!" Her response took me by surprise and was an "other worldliness" that she would express time and time again.

After an argument with a local television station regarded the violent content of their programming and how it might negatively affect the mind of an innocent child, I cancelled my cable and never again reconnected it. It was no loss for Sash though who had a wonderful imagination and replaced the hours she would have spent sitting in front of a box with overflowing creativity and a love of dreaming. She was very conscious of the altered state, sometimes not wanting to wake up in the morning to go to school as a result of being in a really awesome part of a dream. At these times she would gesture for me to go away and to come back later. Upon waking up from one of these dreams she got a pen and piece of paper and proceeded to draw a series of symbols that looked similar to petroglyphs on a rock wall or stone faced ancient building. Her dreamtime experiences were so rich that they reminded me of the aboriginal peoples of Australia.

Sash was connected to the divine which revealed itself through expressions of love that were tossed as if flower bouquets on everyone she touched. As the first grandchild birthed into a family system loaded with the dysfunction and broken heartedness of alcoholism it was this little girl that first introduced the simple words "I love you." These words of love were like a foreign language as they had never been spoken in my childhood home. Love was a teaching she innocently taught us all.

My little girl had a wisdom and an intuitive knowing about people and life that was beyond her years and would often say things that I had no idea how she could know. Her earliest words indicated that she could easily perceive the wounds that people carried, and seemed to have a deep understanding of the importance of love, saying that a person whom I was hurt by or struggling with was needing more love. Interestingly she would not interpret meanness as bullying only tell me the individual "lacked love." As her Mother, my daughter's compassionate an open heart concerned me though because there were bullies in the world. Healing one's heart is a journey requiring personal responsibility and commitment and I felt learning discernment as a form of self-protection would be a life lesson for my little girl.

I was a single parent so my daughter went with everywhere with me, often attending events and workshops. One of these events was an afternoon workshop co-hosted by an indigenous spiritual leader and a local Minister from the Unity Church. The speakers were to take a commonly shared story and interpret it through lens of each spiritual perspective. Before they started their discourse though they led the audience in a grounding exercise which they began with the clanging tone of two brass bells followed by a silent meditation. With my eyes closed I could feel my daughter tugging on my shirt as the group sat in silence. I tried to ignore her, but she kept on tugging on my clothes and whispering to me. I surrendered to her requests and opened my eyes to see her glowing eyes full of light looking back at me. Sash asked for a pen and a piece of paper which I dug out of my bag and handed to her before closing my eyes to go back into the silence A few minutes later, when the meditation was finished I asked her to show me what she had written and she handed me a piece of paper with the following words written on it.

Ha Ha Ha Looa sayuta
Ha Looa sayluta Looa Looa

When I asked her where the words came from she told me that as soon as the bells were rung she began to hear this repeating song singing over and over in her head. She said she had to write it down before she forgot it. I kept the piece of paper with her handwriting on it for twenty years because I sensed she had tapped into an ancient chant sung repeatedly over time, in a holy place on the planet. Although I have yet to research the meanings of the chant my little girl heard and transcribed that day I know in my heart that she entered an ancient spiritual place.

When she was nine years old she informed me that when she feels really angry at me she just sits back and thinks to herself, "Well, I chose this Mom, so I cannot be angry because I made this decision." Pretty radical thinking for a nine year old.

Sascha had an ability to see colors around certain people at certain times and would ask me what the colors meant. She also asked me why the colors on some people, like her teachers, would change on different days. I believed she was seeing the auras surrounding people but I had no idea how to help her integrate this intuitive awareness at such a young age.

My daughter was and is extremely strong willed which often brought parenting challenges and concerns. As her Mother, I struggled over how to protect and nurture such wisdom in a family system and a society that was far too often unconscious of children and young adults and insensitive to their gifts. I made a vow to the Creator when she was born to protect her bright light and to do what was needed within the confines of my own consciousness to achieve this vow.

As Mother and Daughter we certainly went through our relationship struggles but we both found our own way with Sash going on to become a Registered Nurse and becoming a wonderful partner and mother to my two beautiful grandchildren.

Sascha Rose and her son, Nixon Euchere

My Grandson

Five years ago, my daughter gave birth to her son Nixon and I was once again witness to a repeating pattern within our family system. This little boy had big blue eyes and was another wise old soul. Like his Mother, Nixon was connected to his dreams, consciously aware, intuitive and highly sensitive to the emotions and energy of the world around him. He was telepathic and at times, I could see he was hearing and responding to the thoughts of people around him. I had practiced yoga, meditation and Buddhism for over a decade by this time and slowly increasing in my own awareness and sensitivities. As his Grandmother, I was once again concerned regarding how many adults were unaware of their negative thoughts, emotions and conditioned thinking. How could a little boy this sensitive survive in an invisible ocean filled with so much unconsciousness?

For example, I was babysitting Nixon one afternoon while his Mother was out on errands. He was around three years old at the time. We were busy baking cookies and making a good mess when he suddenly looked at me and said, *"Nan, my Mom is coming! We have to go outside and meet her!"* It was winter and rainy and cold outside so I said to him, "Nixon your mom is not coming for another couple of hours." He insisted that this Mom was coming and that we had to go outside and meet her and proceeded to the top of the stairs to gather his boots and to get mine for me to put on.

I surrendered to the moment and willingly stepped into my boots as instructed by my grandson. His hand in mine, I was guided down the stairs, out the door and up through the back yard to the parking lot in the back alley. At the parking lot we both peaked down the alley way to look for his Mom's car, which was nowhere in sight. I then said, "Nixie, your Mom is not coming so let's go back into the house." I was thinking about the cookies and the cold wet winter day. He turned around to face me and said with absolute confidence, "My Mom is coming Nan let's sit down and wait for her." I am still curious and he is my grandson so I say, "Ok" and go and sit down with him on the wooden curb to wait.

We chat for a few moments before I get up to once again to go peak down the alley for his Mom. Just as I am about to announce to Nixon that she is not coming I see her car turn the corner around the blackberry bushes and drive up towards us. I wave to her and tell Nixon his Mom is coming, where upon he jumped up and down for joy and ran a safe distance towards her car. I was completely amazed by this incident. I was amazed by both by his intuition and by his absolute inner confidence in knowing that his Mom was coming early to get him even though she was not expected.

Another time, I was feeling concerned about the well-being of my daughter and grandson while they were away on a road trip. My daughter said that Nixon kept telling his parents that Nan was with them in the car. When the family returned home and my daughter and I were taking Nixon for a walk in the stroller, he turned to me and asked "Nan, why are you in my dreams?" He was only three years old.

Nixon is also tuned into the natural world demonstrating a deep connection and relationship at a very early age. My daughter and I would regularly take him in the stroller for six kilometer walks around a local forested lake. Prior to leaving the forest and out into to the open sky towards the parking lot, Nixon would ask us to stop, then pop out of his stroller and waddle over to the nearest tree, where he would hug the trunk and give thanks to the forest. No one taught him this behavior. He intuitively embodied gratitude, respect and reverence for the natural world and just started hugging trees.

I do not live close by now and therefore, I love to have videos of both my grandchildren when I miss them. On one visit when Nixon was four years old I started up the video and asked him if there was anything he would like to share with the world. In that exact moment he noticed that his shirt was on backwards so he asked if I could give him a second while he fixed his shirt. While waiting for him to switch his shirt I captured his Mom and sister Arianna, all the while thinking that he would likely speak about Spiderman or one of his favorite super hero characters.

Nixon gave me the signal that he was ready to speak so I shifted the camera back towards him and asked if he was ready. Where upon he silently nodded his head and simply said,

"Touch the Earth Gently!"

That was it.

The New Children

I only recently learned about Indigo and Crystal Children, which are the terms used to describe the new children who are born with gifts like my daughter and grandson. It is likely that all our children are born highly sensitive and that our consciousness as parents and grandparents has only recently evolved to the state where we can see our children's gifts. In my own childhood, the conditioning to model your family system was so strong it left very little space to learn and observe your child's true nature with open curiosity.

According to research, Indigos were born between 1970 and 1990, and were given this name because of the indigo aura that could be seen around them. Indigo children demonstrate a higher state of human evolution and have a telepathic ability to read minds. These children have a special wisdom and a profound sense of compassion. With their heightened sensitivity and compassion comes an ability to heal which wounded people can sense and are drawn to. These gifted children are strong willed with warrior like spirits that command alignment with their truth. A combination that can lead to challenges for parents. These willful warriors make excellent leaders though, and who often use their gifts and passions to challenge outdated illusions that no longer serve life on earth.

In the early 1990s professionals started noticing the birth of children with different qualities whom they called, Crystal Children. These children are said to be balanced in both the left and right hemispheres of the brain. They are highly sensitive and tend to have big beautiful eyes that will stare directly into your soul leading to the sense of being seen. Like Indigos they also have the ability to communicate telepathically, making them highly sensitive to the thought patterns of those around them. They often speak about past lives, the stars and planets or other worlds beyond earth. Crystal children are like little jolly Buddha's, who are very forgiving and are natural born healers. My grandson Nixon has the biggest blue eyes that are filled with crystalline structures, and interesting that I used to lovingly call him my little Buddha. These children are lucid dreamers retaining the information received while in dream states. Crystal children have a clear sense of knowing and have internal truth detectors, or GPS systems that they trust to guide and show them the way.

I truly hope that we as parents and grandparents become more conscious of our children's sensitivities and collectively work towards nurturing their gifts into full fruition. Our children are born intuitive, wise and naturally connected to the truth of their own soul and the natural world. As adults, many of the blocks we struggle to dissolve while striving to reconnect with our natural intuitive state are false beliefs placed there by ourselves, our family and society.

From the perspective of intuitive development there is a gap here that can be bridged with more awareness. It seems like such a great loss of human potential, and we are in need of out of the box creative ideas, compassion and wisdom if we are going to transform and evolve in consciousness.

Elders: Our Wisdom Keepers

There were two Elders in my life who were pivotal in shaping my beliefs and ideas regarding intuitive intelligence. One of these women was my Great Granny with the Birds and the other, is my dear Auntie Nan who is known for her psychic abilities and healing touch.

My Aunt

It was to Auntie Nan's table for a cup of tea and an intimate talk family members would often go when struggling with a life challenge. A conversation with Auntie Nan was always nourishing to the soul. She listened deeply and had what I would call today "presence." My Auntie Nan was compassionate, non-judgmental, and accepting of all and for me, she embodied a rare kind of wisdom.

She was born with psychic gifts and known for her prophetic dreams, intuitive insights and for the voices that spoke to her that were not her own. These voices and visions often occurred when one of the people she loved was at risk; be it health, personal or activity related. It is recalled by her family that when she was born the nurses came into the room and whispered to my grandmother that her baby daughter was born with a halo around her, something rarely seen in newborns.

Due to a lack of understanding or mentors to teach my aunt how to use her gift she eventually blocked off her abilities. I lovingly refer to her as the reluctant psychic. When I asked why she would want to cut off such a gift she simply replied that she often knew things that she could do nothing about. This kind of knowing often caused her to suffer, as awareness can be a profound responsibility and she felt powerless to create change. This said, I am aware that as a result of the voices and visions my Aunt was able to intervene at times and change the course of the future. For example, while doing the dishes she heard a voice tell her that her young grandsons were in trouble and she saw that they had climbed onto the roof of her house which was set on a hill. Upon hearing and seeing them in her mind's eye she was able to go directly to them and guide them off the roof before they risked falling and physically injuring themselves. I am sure there were many times she received information that she could do nothing about though and this made her heart heavy.

In leadership it is said that our greatest strength can also be our greatest challenge. In my Aunt's case she was gifted with phenomenal psychic abilities but did not have a mentor to teach her how to manage or how to cope with the information she often received. I could understand how painful her psychic vision must have been at times. Increased awareness also brings with it an increased levels of responsibility. A responsibility and weight that not everyone wants to walk with in their everyday life. Witnessing and understanding the challenges that my Aunt experienced highlights the importance of growing slowly in intuitive awareness with adequate learning resources, mentoring, guidance and support.

Great Granny with the Birds

I sat straight up in bed. What was this stuff I was reading?

It was past eleven at night and my little girl was sound asleep in the room beside me. I had been reading what was supposed to be my Great Grandmother's poetry journal. I am a lover of poetry and had been given a couple of my Great Grandmother's journals by my Granny because of our shared love of language. Reading through the words on the pages I could feel the spirit world coming in far closer than I desired. The reality of her written words were bringing up a mixture of both awe and fear. Fear of the unknown and awe for the sense of an unseen power and intelligence that I could feel all around me as I read each page. I closed the journal, got up out of bed and turned on all of the lights. As I sat there on my bed in the light of darkness, and began returning to my comfort zone I started scanning my own thoughts and memories.

Besides being the woman whom I lovingly referred to as *"Great Granny with the Birds,"* who exactly was this woman? At the time of my initial reading she had been gone for over a decade. I knew that she was a healer and prolific writer and from the words I had just read, she was a whole lot more complex. I was curious and knew that I needed to learn more about her and her life. To my knowledge she had never achieved any greatness academically, but without a higher education how could she make sense out of what she wrote so freely about? Her journal contained advanced concepts in science, quantum physics, spirituality, psychology and astronomy. Concepts that I didn't really even understand, nor had I heard of spiritualism or channelling at the time of first reading. I was aware that she was different and could feel that she had another kind of knowing. Even as a little girl I remembered this sense of other worldliness and mystery around her.

The wise words I read that night, over thirty years ago now, were to take me on a long journey of discovery. A journey of discovery about myself, my ancestry, my family and the mysterious world inhabited by my Great Granny with the Birds along with similar cultures and wisdom traditions. It became a spiritual journey of an unexpected sort. A journey into an unseen dimension of reality that appeared to have disappeared from within my family system, and socially with the affluence of our materialistic times and the emphasis on economic growth. Or perhaps this spiritual presence was still very much alive but had shape shifted into different forms?

Her Life

My Great Grandmother was born in England but immigrated to Canada in her early twenties where she met and married my Great Grandfather. My Great Grandfather was a soldier in the British army and served in India, and then later in Africa where he was wounded in battle. He returned to the family home on the west coast of Canada to recover, where he remained until his death. My Great Grandfather passed from this world long before I was born, and I consider myself blessed to have met and to still have memories of my Great Grandmother.

She lived in their beautiful old English home just a block from Gonzales Bay in Victoria, British Columbia and from time to time, our family would drive down from our farm in Cobble Hill to visit her. My earliest childhood memories are of walking along a path through a lovely old English garden brimming with beautiful flowers, herbs, vegetables, song birds and the buzzing of insects.

At the doorway we would be met by a tiny little old lady in a frock, thick stockings and black shoes (I always loved her black lace up shoes with the funky heals) who would escort our family up the stairs and into her kitchen to be served tea. There were three bird cages in the kitchen with canaries who sang their little hearts out while we sipped tea and to whom she chatted to with as if close friends throughout the duration of our visit. It was through this relationship with her canaries that she acquired the nickname of *"Great Granny with the Birds"* and even her own physical body was bird like.

As a little girl I sensed there was something different about my Great Grandmother and as I grew up I began to hear more and more stories about her and how crazy she was. I was often told that I was a lot like her and although I have embraced this idea today, at the time I wasn't sure if this comment was meant as a compliment or a judgement upon me. Like many people with a gift my Great Grandmother was unfortunately stigmatized and ridiculed by some family members whom I'm sure had no understanding of her psychic abilities, nor the degree of her intelligence. You knew when you met her that she was different, but to my knowledge, she kept the spiritual aspects of herself fairly well hidden when in good health. However, as she got older the boundaries defining her physical and spiritual world became blurred. As a result, she would often say things that were not understood especially given the context of some people's reality. As her health declined the stories of her craziness increased. I remembered this as I read through her journal and got a greater grasp of her gifts and felt very sad for our social immaturity and for the limitations of human awareness that lead to the kinds of attacks she received at her life's end.

Through my research I learned that she belonged to the International Order of Spiritualists, an organization with chapters all over the world, and that she was a channeler, healer, psychic, intellect, poet and prolific writer. Spiritualism was very popular during this era. From her daughter, my Granny, it was confirmed that she had a healing room in her house. I remember that room to this day as it actually had a crystal set in the center of a table and was filled with plants. Spiritualism was popular in her day with many famous people venturing into the unseen world as explorers of consciousness and sharing their experiences openly with the world. As a result, several prominent politicians and business people were regular visitors to my Great Grandmother's home, coming to see her for healings and channeled readings. It was this world that I entered upon receiving and reading my Great Grandmother's journals.

My Grandmothers Journals

While stationed in India as a soldier during the British rule, my Great Grandfather became acquainted with the mystic, Rabindranath Tagore. It was a connection that grew into a friendship and a relationship that both my Grandparents maintained upon their relocation to Canada, and that my Grandmother kept even after my Grandfathers death. Her journals were filled with writings from this mystic, who was a man that remained a mystery to me for over a decade after reading his words for the first time. Tagore and his mysticism became an integral part of my discovery of my Great Grandmother's world. Although I will not go into detail about this great man, he was also an explorer of the creative impulse and deeply connected to the earth and to spirit.

Rabindranath Tagore, was a Hindu Nobel Laureate known for his prolific writing, poetry and divine visions. He was a Universalist and a world renowned speaker who quit school in his primary years; taking his future school lessons in the garden of his family's estate. Many spiritual leaders today like Deepak Chopra still reference Tagore's mystical writings in their books and during speaking engagements.

As I read through my Great Grandmother's journals I realized that she embodied knowledge that was beyond my comprehension at that time. She channeled angelic beings and wrote about interconnectedness, atoms, energy, quantum physics, matter and spirit. The content of my Great Grandmother's journals contributed to my curiosity regarding the relationship of human beings within the living fabric of the universe and to other ways of knowing.

The following pages contain a glimpse of my Great Grandmother's channeled writings as I read them in her journal over thirty years ago, along with a couple of excerpts from the International Spiritualist Review. All of the words were transcribed from a tattered black notebook filled with my Grandmother's handwriting as scribed in her old style blue ink fountain pen.

Wisdom down the Ages

You see, everything is considered here, even the things which seem so casual and transitory in the earth life.

They are all registered in relation to one another, all the seemingly casual talks, or chance meetings; a book read, a hand-shaken in the street for the first time and never again, or a few friends meeting in the same way at a mutual friends house and never meeting again—everything and every item is registered, considered, coordinated and used when and if, occasion offers.

Be therefore, not remiss to weigh well all you do and every word you say; not in anxiety, but rather by cultivating a habit of will to do good.

Always and everywhere to radiate kindness of heart, for in the kingdom these are not of small account, but go to make spirits bright and bodies radiant.

The spirits of the discarnate workers speaking.
Astriel

Spirit & Matter

Thus you can see how intimate the relationship is between spirit and matter. When the other evening we spoke of your own church building and the allotting of guardians and workers among other things, for the care of the material edifice, we were only telling you of the same principle at work on a smaller scale. The scheme which provides for the upkeep of all those millions of suns and their planets took note also of the re-arrangement of certain congeries (collections) of atoms—some in the form of stone, others wood and brick—which resulted in that new entity you call a church. These are held together, each atom in its place, by the outflowing power of will. They are not placed there and left solitary, were this done, the building would soon crumble away and fall to pieces.

Now in the light of what we have written, think about what people call "the difference of feeling" on entering a church, or theatre, or dwelling house, or any building. Each has its own emanations, and these are a consequence of the same principle at work, which we have tried to describe. It is the spirit speaking through the medium of the material particles and their arrangement and purpose to the spirits of those who enter that place.

Astriel
Channeled Communication

Spiritual Guides

More over friend, it is a good thing and helpful to bear in mind our presence at all times; for we are near, and that in ways both many and various. When we are personally near at hand we are able to impress you with helpful thoughts and intuitions, and so to order events that your work may be facilitated, and your way made clearer than it otherwise would appear to you. When in person we are in our own spheres, we still have means whereby we are informed not alone of what has happened in and around you, but also what is about to happen, if the composition of circumstances is to pursue its normal course.

Thus preserving contact with you, we maintain and ensure our guardianship that it be continuous and unceasing, and our watchfulness is that it shall in no way fail on your behalf. For here and through the spheres between you and us, are contingencies by which intelligence is sent on from one sphere to those beyond, and when necessity requires it, we inform others to carry out some mission to you, or if the occasion so requires, we come to earth ourselves, as I have done this time. But further still, and in addition to this, we are able to come into contact with his own charge direct in certain ways, and to influence events from our own place.

Channeled Communication

Soul in Science

There was a time when science did not mean what it means today to humankind; when there was a soul in science, and the outer manifestation in matter was a secondary interest. Thus it was with alchemy, astrology and even engineering.

It was known in those days, that the world was ruled from many spheres, and ministered to by countless hosts of servants acting freely of their own will, but within certain straight limits laid down by those of greater power, and higher authority.

Men in those days studied to find out the different grades and degrees of those spiritual workers, and the manner of their service in the different departments of nature and of human life, and the amount of power exercised by each several class.

They found out a considerable number of facts, and classified them, but in as much as these facts, laws and regulations and conditions were not of the earth sphere but of the spiritual, they were fain to express them in a language apart from common use.

Channeled Communication

Loss of Soul

When another generation grew up whose energies were directed in other ways than these, not considering well what manner of knowledge was contained in the love of their ancestors, said the language was allegorical or symbolic: and thus doing, they also made the facts themselves assume a shadowy form, until at last there was little of the reality left.

Thus it happened with regard to the study of the spiritual powers of varying degree and race and this issued into the fairy tales of Europe, and the magic stories of the East.

These are really the lineal and legitimate descendants of the science of the past, added to, subtracted from, and distorted in many ways. And yet, if you study and read these fairy tales in the light of what I have said, you will see that, when you have separated the essentials from the more modern embroidering there are to be found there, embedded like the cities of Egypt under the sands of the ages, solid facts of science, or knowledge as spiritually considered.

Channeled Communication

Inspiration

Inspiration, therefore, is of wide meaning and extent of practice. The prophets of the old time, and those of today—received our instruction according to the quickening of their faculties. Some were able to hear our words, some able to see us—both as to their spiritual bodies—others were impressed mentally. These and other ways do we employ, and all to the one end, namely; to impact through them to their fellow men instruction as to the way they should go, and in what way they should order their lives to please God, as we are able to understand his will from this higher plane. Our council is not of perfection, nor infallible, but it never leads astray those who seek worthily and with much prayer and great love.

These are God's own, and they are a great joy to his fellow servants. Nor need we go far afield to find them, for there is more good in the world than evil, and as in each, good and evil is proportioned, so we are able to help, and so is our ability limited.

So do everyone these two things—see that your light is kept burning as they who wait for the Lord, for it is his will we do in this matter, and it is his strength we bring. Prayers are allotted us to answer, and his answer is sent by us his servants. So be watchful and wakeful for our coming, we who are of those who came to him in the wilderness, and in Yethsimgne, albeit I think they would be of a higher degree than I.

And another to bear in mind is this, see you keep your motive high and noble, and seek not selfishly, but for others welfare. We minister best to the progress of those who seek our help for the benefit of their brethren rather than their own.

Channeled Communication

Spiritualism

At the time of birth, the essence of who we are, our Spirit, enters into the physical or earthly world. During life these two bodies, physical and spiritual, are linked together. When we die the link is severed and our material body is returned to the Earth. However, our spiritual being continues on. Our Spirit, or Essence, as I like to refer to it, carries our character from life to life.

What we do in each life determines what awaits us in the Spirit world, and in future lives. If we have acted with good will and kindness, we will be rewarded in our spiritual status. This, in effect, is true to the meaning of 'cause and effect' or 'what you sow, so shall you reap.'

The spiritual world surrounds us, and is not in a faraway place. It is a world governed by love that operates on a variety of levels. Much of the spirit world is not comprehensible to many people, as it cannot be seen, nor heard. We as human beings are limited in our sensory abilities due to the restraints of our physical bodies. For example, we can only hear at a certain frequency and our sight can only provide us with a certain range of vision. There are however, certain highly sensitive individuals that are able to sense what others fail to perceive.

I believe all of us are born with a certain amount of this sensitivity, but often during the process of childhood these gifts are not recognized and developed. Instead the natural tendency of western culture is to repress these abilities. In many indigenous cultures, uniqueness is recognized and nurtured into fruition, but in western culture expressions that do not fit into the culturally determined norm are crushed until we end up walking around in fear of discovery.

God is not a white man. God is not even a person. God is the Creative Universal Spirit that exists everywhere and in everything. Including in each and every one of us. Every human being is divine because we each carry a spark of divinity in our heart. The reason for discovering our own spirituality is so we can connect at the deepest level with our divine purpose, or path in life. When we meditate, spend quiet time in nature or do the things we need to do to feel and to hear our personal message we journey into a process of unique self-discovery. It is in this place that we can ask the questions we so long ago stopped asking with the trust that our questions would be answered.

Journal Note
Great Granny with the Birds

Unto Thee Creator: Do We Give Thanks

Creator of a vast Universe of Life and living Light—Giver and Preserver of all creatures great and small, visible and invisible, importing the Spirit of Life into seeds of production which descend in particles from that wonderful store-house of Divine Love and Wisdom, passing down from sphere to sphere, leaving a part of the intellectual light of the spirit dimmed as it intermingles with lower elements on its downward mission, then for a period dwelling in darkness. Then, with the aid of invisible forces of creation, it forms a covering for the spirit to dwell in, lighting up again into a vast sea of living life.

The mystic voice of inspiration guides it into the realm of thought where FAITH is the foundational energy. Hope is the eternal existence of the spiritual life and CHARITY the spirit of love, cooperating through the unseen in all pathways of creation, sending forth its rays into a wonderful wave of light which expands as it draws in new knowledge of its higher ascent and destination toward the great dawn, when the spirit shall breathe in the essence of its counterpart, holding fast to the eternal Rock of Ages in which it was created—crying out in thankfulness to the Supreme Divine Architect of All Creation.

International Spiritualist Review

Progress of Human Intellect

There are many worlds in the vast Universe, with people in varying stages of evolution; thus it is with our own planet. Humankind must progress and discover new knowledge to utilize the great natural resources that God has placed upon this planet for human use.

So, as human's progress, they are granted further knowledge to make new discoveries, so that they may progress. Always the necessary discoveries are presented to them as they progress. According to this DIVINE dispensation, prophets are prepared, and philosophers raised up to open up the way for these necessary discoveries, a Chaldean Seer to dispense a revelation of the Creation; a Grecian to define moral philosophy, a Jesus to show man his Spiritual purpose and purer conception of the Supreme; a Newton, a Galileo, and a Franklin to open up new scientific possibilities to humankind.

The great chain of Spirit's influence continues unbroken; without it humankind would perish, like plants if denied sunlight. Therefore, the minds of humans must ever be open to receive the Truth, ever ready to receive new ideas and knowledge, free to judge and compare as their power of comprehension develops, but never fatally closed to the acceptance of New Truths.

International Spiritualist Review

Mother Earth
Our Home in the Universe

Mother Earth
Our Home in the Universe

My childhood sense of interconnectedness with nature led me to commit a decade of my adult life working in sustainable community development collaborating on transformational programs and projects such as alternative transportation, composting, naturescaping and urban farming to name just a few. I believed in my heart that the sense of interconnectedness that I felt as a little girl was being forgotten and lost, leading to far greater losses that could sometimes be seen and felt but not entirely understood.

As I stepped forward I found myself surrounded by many other passionate activists and change makers: protecting through reconnecting to the wonders of our glorious home on Mother Earth. A planet known in ancient times as Gaia; a living being that is conscious, life sustaining, self-regulating, powerful, rich in diversity and exquisitely beautiful.

Over the past decade, I redirected my focus towards First Nation's peoples and their communities. Based upon what I knew with regards to my consulting in sustainable development I felt the indigenous worldview was important to understand and therefore, I approached my work as a student of learning. Opening up my heart to the indigenous lens, to their visionary abilities and holistic seventh generation thinking, to their connection to the land, and spiritual traditions and their quiet centered wisdom. I often feel more at home in indigenous cultures than in my own, as the people still embodied a deeper sense of knowing about Mother Earth and the Great Spirit, a landscape and reality that most of modern society seemed to have long ago forgotten.

I was also curious about their intuitive leadership style and their sacred relationship with the web of life, along with their understandings of both the visible and invisible realms of creation. I had heard the Elder's stories so many times about the richness of the world they lived in before the white man came. Rivers so thick with fish, you could literally walk across their backs to the land on the other side. I wanted to learn more about why the indigenous voice had become silenced and if there was any connection to the world we are currently at risk of losing. Through my work as a consultant, I learned about the intercultural challenges the people faced in order to rise above the forces of oppression, embedded racism, and healing from the intergenerational traumas of residential school.

Mother Earth is our home and from outer space we can easily see that there are no firm boundaries separating the air, water and land, nor wildlife, wild spaces and people. Not long ago, I asked a young man on a bus where he was from and he looked at me with confusion and a mischievous smile and said, "Mother Earth, where are you from?" I found wisdom in his youthful response.

Our planet and home is intimately connected to all the celestial bodies in our Universe. The stars, the planets, our sun and our moon and all of the other bodies in the vast space have a profound influence on the earth and existence. The circling of the sun, the pull of the moon on the tides of the ocean and women's menstrual cycles are just a few of the more obvious invisible forces. There is a sacred balance that is maintained through celestial cycles, rhythms and invisible forces that enable life to flourish on Mother Earth.

The Problem

In a very short timeframe our global human family has risen to a population of 7 billion. All the while we have been consuming, extracting and polluting more than earth's resources are able to sustain. According to the vision as given to me by the ancient feminine presence, and as evidenced by the number of environmental and social disasters occurring more and more frequently on our planet, there are valid concerns regarding the state of our planet and her ability to sustain life.

Nations and beliefs are pushing in upon each other and fear, violence and war is becoming more common place. Government and corporate corruption and exploitation of the masses is no longer hidden, and has become known by young and old, right and left, developing nations and over developed nations. Censorship is increasingly being enforced that infringes upon privacy rights and our freedom of expression. Science and technology has taken over and left the human heart out of the equation. We need a new kind of leadership that integrates the heart and mind, bringing forth wisdom and holistic visionary thinking. We need a new vision and a new dream of earth because the old forms of leadership are galloping humanity blindly towards the edge of a cliff.

The sky watchers of the ancient world that once observed the heavens for celestial signs would today see planes crisscrossing our sky, leaving behind white trails that stretch from horizon to horizon. Trails in the sky containing unknown chemicals that pollute the soil we grow our food in, the air we all breathe and the water we drink. This program is known as geoengineering which is a technology developed for the purpose of weather modification. Governing agencies insist that geoengineering is only in the research stages, but the evidence in the sky and the declining health of our natural systems indicates another story.

Other concerns the ancients would observe in our world today include:

- Science and technology being used to produce genetically modified seeds that negatively affect human health. Pesticides that poison the soil and the beneficial insects and plants that make up the food we eat.
- Antiquated energy systems that extract what is referred to as dirty energy, because the technology uses a finite resource that pollutes the air, water and land with clean energy sources being repressed.
- Trees, bees and wild creatures dying off in alarming rates.
- Corporations dominating global society through the misuse of wealth, power and media.
- News media increasingly headlining the violence and rape of young women in nations all over the world.
- Regional disasters such as flooding, tsunamis, tornados and super storms have become common place.

The list is endless.

Media, television and Hollywood are producing a steady stream of movies and images that enter into our consciousness foretelling the destruction of the planet and all of life. The visual reality that is being downloaded into our minds through mainstream media far too often resembles a nightmare. Lacking the visionary potential of humanity for wisdom, peace, respect, compassion and creativity.

The problems we face today in both human and earth systems are extremely complex. The vision I received from the Grandmothers was a calling to reach for a higher platform of consciousness in order to transform the pending collapse of our home on Mother Earth from the false beliefs currently directing the course of reality.

The Mayan Calendar predicted that the end of a great cosmic cycle would occur on December 21, 2012. This date is said to herald in the beginning of new cosmic cycle requiring a shift into higher state of consciousness. Humanity has been going through this "shift" for many decades, but according to the Mayan cosmology, 2009 was the start of the really big changes and the birthing of a new mystical consciousness built upon ecology, care of the environment and care of each other.

Losing Our Connection to Living Systems

We exist within a living fabric, a web of life that is interconnected and made up of wholes upon wholes, similar to the idea proposed in the wonderful storybook "Horton Hears a Who" by Dr. Suess where life is enfolded within life. Each living system affects all the other living systems that it is connected to, either consciously or unconsciously. Unfortunately, humanity has been conditioned to believe that we are separate and disconnected from this sacred web of life. Through a fragmentation of thinking our mind, body and spirit have also become fragmented into disconnected parts of a whole energy field. We have forgotten that we are in continuous communication with our internal Self and our external world, and that the laws of karma are natural laws affecting the well-being of ourselves and Mother Earth. We are interconnected living systems of Creation.

Our planet has been ruled by patriarchy, Newtonian Science and the Industrial Revolution for centuries now which has created a belief system of reality as a mechanical machine. This machine is devoid of life and is an ideology that has become the foundation from which we have constructed our current reality. The results are what we see and experience today in economic methodologies such as factory farming for meat, fruit and vegetables. A style of farming that is focused on the singular goal of accumulating financial wealth, and not of sustaining the living systems co-creating our nourishment.

I grew up on a mixed farm where we raised chickens, pigs and cows and harvested vegetables from our garden, and fruit and nuts from our orchard. Every odd season our fruit trees would become severely infested with caterpillars. Although we would try to minimize the impact upon our fruit trees, the underlying belief was that this was part of the natural order of nature. As a little girl, I was told that the caterpillars left a chemical residue on the tree that was necessary for its protection within its whole life cycle of the tree and the orchard. This was a symbiotic relationship that had developed over eons of time between both the tree and the caterpillar. Each organism contributing to the wellness of the other through symbiosis—a long term cycle ensuring the harmonious health of the other. This is an example of an interconnected living system based upon sacred relationship.

These kinds of relationships are part of the natural order, and examples can be found everywhere in nature. Factory farming methodologies look at short term goals that maximize production for profit but the entire exchange is without the awareness of the consciousness of life. It is an organizational structure devoid of heart and soul and is rooted in our fragmented thinking, being and doing. Nature has a natural intuitive intelligence that operates in long term cycles to maximize harmony and wellness for the entire web of life.

Layered on top of these beliefs of fragmentation is the loss of the feminine presence in decision making, leadership and knowledge creation. The loss of the feminine voice has contributed to the loss of balance in conscious co-creation as the feminine is connected to the Great Mystery through her life giving properties and consciousness. A way of being and seeing that ensures a continual thread is cast out into our children's world and the world future generations will inhabit.

Collectively these perceptions have led to a reality where life has lost its sense of sacredness, magic, mystery and spirit. It is my belief that the loss of the feminine has also affected our ability to understand indigenous peoples who remain connected to the Earth Mother, along with our attitudes towards children and gay males who are more comfortable with the feminine within, which is within us all.

Our disconnection from the sacred spirit flowing through our bodies and the earth is the mechanism that enables the destructive behaviors on earth to continue. We have forgotten our sense of wholeness or holiness, and from a place of disconnection we become cut off from our feelings, and unable to comprehend the harm caused by our behavior. The material world is here for our physical experience and enjoyment, but we need a conscious way of producing these goods and services that benefits and enhances life for the whole living system involved in co-creation.

The Loss of the
Sacred Feminine

In my own life it was predominantly the woman who carried the gift of intuition, with the exception of my Grandson. Although men are obviously intuitive, the social conditioning they receive as little boys is far harsher, resulting in a greater loss of their inherent sensitivities. The idea that big boys don't cry has a profound and lasting impact upon grown men, often leaving them disconnected from their feelings and carrying a false belief that they need to be tough to be real men. Many of these same men occupy our predominantly male organizational systems where they are in leadership positions and in control of the world's governance, decision-making and knowledge creation. Leaving an obvious gap in the feminine worldview and the ability of the feminine to influence important spheres including governance, decision making and knowledge creation as well as the well-being and future of our children, our interconnectedness with nature and reality as known through our heart and our emotions.

Through my research I discovered that there was a time in our common story when the Mother Goddess reigned for her divine wisdom, and was respected for her intuitive knowledge and her connection to the mystery. Gradually, over time and significant events this social stature was lost, making it unsafe to express women's wisdom and the intuitive voice.

Archeological excavations have uncovered Goddess figurines throughout most of ancient Europe, but these symbols eventually disappear completely from the artifacts of time. The primeval Mother Goddess of the primitive world was the ancient feminine presence of earth, also known as Gaia. The Mother Goddess was seen as being at one with nature and the giver of life who roamed the wild woods and inhabited dark spaces. Through the cycles of her own body, she was connected to the entire cycle of life and to the mysterious invisible dimensions. She was the Great Mother, the Big Mama who danced with life and death and the divine, maintaining a cosmic balance between both the seen, and the unseen dimensions of space.

The loss of the feminine is first initiated with the biblical story of Adam and Eve, and peaks again just before the birth of Christ. During this time period a great power struggle ensued between the many Gods and the Goddesses. A battle where the Gods were victorious resulting in a societal demotion of the Goddess, the feminine presence. After this loss in stature, societies began accumulating wealth and warring civilizations began to arise in the historical records that were based upon competition, violence, domination and control.

Although the removal of the Mother Goddess began long before birth of Christ, the war against women peaked sharply from the 15th to the 18th century with the infamous witch trials and the torture and execution of thousands of women. There were no hospitals, doctors or clinics in villages throughout Europe in this era, and even though these women were wise healers and midwives, embodying a vast knowledge of medicinal plants, some of their practices were considered magical, mysterious and supernatural. Collectively this kind of power invoked fear of the unknown in many sectors of society, including within the church and state.

It is difficult to know for sure the exact number of women who were killed during this period, as records were rarely kept in many European countries. Estimates of the numbers of witches tried and executed range from as high as nine million to around forty five thousand women. Both figures are substantially high and either way, it is a massive assault upon women and women's ways of knowing. When reflecting upon the impacts of the collective terror from this period, it is important to acknowledge the many courageous men who also lost their lives for speaking out against the atrocious crimes cast upon woman.

The resulting traumas from this era still live in our collective unconscious and can be felt through a residual energy of fear. A fear I briefly felt, but did not understand at the onset of researching and writing my thesis on *"Intuition & Leadership: The Art of Wise Decision-Making"* during graduate studies. This collective fear continues to influence our freedom to openly share women's ways of knowing and the intuitive voice in men, women and children. Much like the indigenous peoples of today who for the past century were forced to take their earth based spiritual traditions underground as governments throughout the world declared the practices illegal.

This collective fear has also influenced current cultural beliefs and assumptions regarding the value of women and girls through the world. Dehumanizing beliefs remain in the human psyche that objectify the feminine leading to the rape and violence of women, both young and old along with a degree of social acceptance. This issue has been rising to the surface in places such as New Delhi, India, where a 23 year old student was gang raped on a bus by six men and died three days later in hospital. The country is still mourning the loss of this young woman a year later, and trying to come to grips with why this level of violence is occurring so frequently. In my own country, Rehteah Parsons from Nova Scotia was gang raped by four young men at the age of 15 and then later bullied through online photographs and tormenting comments. The intense suffering this sensitive young woman endured caused her to commit suicide at the age of 17. Reteah's Mother has been speaking out publicly, and drawing attention to her daughter's story as a means of influencing social change and bringing honor and dignity to her daughter's life. These are only a couple of the many stories that made headlines over the past year indicating a serious problem in social beliefs and attitudes regarding the status of the feminine in the collective consciousness. Thought patterns that I believe are also transferred onto Mother Earth, with the penetration of her physical being to extract her resources solely for profit, and when more sustainable technologies are available but repressed. The feminine in both cases is objectified with a lack of apparent awareness regarding inherent value.

In more recent times, the "Craft of the Wise" is the name given to those previously known of as witches. A more appropriate title, because these women were in tune with the forces of nature and the village healers, midwives, seers and shamans. These wisdom keepers embodied a wealth of knowledge regarding the invisible and unseen dimensions of reality, along with medicinal plants and their healing and psychological properties for communion with the spirit world: or the Great Mystery, the Divine, the God/Goddess or the Creator.

In my own lifetime, my Great Granny with the Birds, my Aunt, my daughter and perhaps even my Grandson could have been considered a witch within the fear based consciousness of the fifteenth century. Witches, Wise Women or Wild Women observed people, the natural world and wildlife and spent time in silence. They listened to the trees and the plants, heard messages in the songs of birds, felt the vibrations in the land, talked to animals, communed with nature spirits and listened to the voice of the wind and the water. They knew without knowing how they knew, because they were and are tuned in to the invisible realms and knew they were a part of all that is. There is no doubt that this communion is a great mystery, but it is not a mystery to be feared because it is a gift from the Creator. A gift we are all born into this world with in varying degrees, but gradually lose over time as we become more separated from our heart, and from our sense of wholeness or holiness.

Today we have the Wiccan and Pagan faiths which still practice the "Spirit of Oneness" and the ideology that the God/Goddess is everywhere, in everyone and in everything: including in the trees, the flowers, the land, the sea and sky. Individuals following these beliefs maintain a deep respect and reverence for Mother Nature, integrating her cycles and rhythms with the understanding that these energies must be kept in balance in order for life to flourish abundantly. One of the most famous woman of modern times is Starhawk (http://www.starhawk.org) who has written numerous books on earth based spirituality and has a movie coming out shortly called, "The Fifth Sacred Thing."

The Paradigm Shift

Humanity is shifting away from one way of being based upon a certain code of shared beliefs and values into another way of perceiving and participating in the world, a social process which is commonly known of as a Paradigm Shift. The term Paradigm Shift was first introduced by Thomas Kuhn in his book, *"The Structure of Scientific Revolutions"* which is an overview of the transition from one worldview to another; arising as a result of the infusion of new knowledge that contradicts the existing values and beliefs. In the language of leadership, humanity is releasing old antiquated beliefs such as power by force, competition, control, manipulation, corruption, and the exploitation of resources solely for profit. The current degradation of human and environmental systems is the physical evidence that our old worldview no longer has the capacity to sustain or support life, bringing us to a crossroads. One path is leading humanity towards destruction, and the other path requires new dreams that integrate innovation, creativity and collaborative conversation.

Collectively we are contributing to the destructive course of this fading reality through our silent participation, although new structures are arising all the time that embody innovations rooted in holistic thinking. The guiding values of the new dream will be based upon interconnectedness or unity consciousness, a realization of the sacredness of all life, respect for nature, integrity, transparency, equality and cooperation. The following table provides a sample of the shift in values and beliefs between the current paradigm and the emerging worldview.

Old Worldview	A New Dream
Competition	Cooperation
Hierarchy	Equality
Domination & Authority	Respect, Collaboration & Co-creation
Exploitation of Life for Profit	Sacredness of All Life
Separation & Fragmentation	Interconnectedness, Wholeness & Unity
Secrets & Lies	Transparency & Truth
Fear	Love
Violence & War	Safety & Peace
Exclusion	Inclusive—Embracing Diversity
Conflict	Cooperation & Harmony
Ridicule & Criticism	Acceptance, Open Communication, Curiosity, Deep Listening
Manipulation	Authenticity & Truth
Minimize Human Potential	Maximize Human Potential
Patriarchy: Masculine Worldview	Integrated Masculine & Feminine
Repression & Oppression	Freedom
Mechanical Universe—Non Living & Non Feeling	A Living Universe— Participatory & Vibrantly Alive

This list is by no means complete, but provides an example of the transformation of values and beliefs connected to this Paradigm Shift, and the emerging changes in our perceptual worldview. Notice that the consciousness emitted from the left side of the table is of a low vibrational frequency, where the consciousness emitted from the New Dream embodies energy of a much higher frequency and closer to the heart and to love. This shift is impacting and influencing all living systems, organizations and disciplines at this time in evolution. As a result, external sources of authority can no longer be accepted as absolute truth because the foundation that the old worldview is built upon no longer sustains life on Mother Earth.

The greatest innovators and geniuses throughout time have trusted intuitively inspired wisdom to guide them to answers once thought impossible, and this same gift is available to every individual for empowered living. Intuition can be nurtured in our children, our families and organizations making intuitively inspired knowledge more accessible through open communication and curiosity. We all have an inner guru, genie or genius available if we choose to tune in, ask and listen for the response of the Universe.

Intuitive leadership is another way of knowing and being, an alternative pathway to knowledge that is too often repressed in our society and therefore, invisible within our problem solving equations. This is just one path amongst many during these co-creative times of change. According to Einstein and many other geniuses our intuition is a forgotten gift. A gift of wise council, available to all those who believe in other forms of knowing, dreaming decision-making and problem solving.

Unity Consciousness

A human being is a part of the whole, called by us "Universe." He experiences himself, his thoughts and feelings as something separated from the rest as a kind of optical delusion of his consciousness. This delusion is a kind of prison for us, restricting us to our personal desires and to affection for a few persons nearest to us. Our task must be to free ourselves from this prison by widening our circle of compassion to embrace all living creatures and the whole of nature in its beauty."

Albert Einstein

Bridging Worldviews

Ancient & New Science

The Living Earth

I simply had not noticed this gift back where I grew up, since other animals and plants were not acknowledged as sentient beings capable of creative expression. But in traditional and tribal communities I found myself among people who practiced paying attention to the polyvalent speech of the landscape assumed to be quivering with intelligence, who regularly turned to the sensitive's among them to interpret the land's gestures. Here, such empaths were valued for their ability to dialogue with the living earth and its animal powers.

Most of the medicine persons who I met were precisely such individuals, whose sensitive nature empowered them to tend the boundary between the human collective and the local earth. By communicating through their propitiations and their chants, through their dances and ecstatic trances with plants, with other animals and with the visible and invisible elements, the medicine persons' craft ensured that the boundary between the human and the more than human worlds stayed itself permeable—that that boundary never hardened into a barrier, but remained a porous membrane across which nourishment flowed steadily in both directions.

David Abram
Becoming Animal: An Earthly Cosmology

Bridging Worlds

To gain insight into the world of intuition, and it's role in the paradigm shift, and dreaming new dreams, we will begin by transcending the spectrums of time and consciousness. Ancient wisdom is a look into the world of our ancestors through the perspectives of indigenous knowledge, mysticism and shamanism. For the purpose of this conversation New Science is leading edge research in quantum physics that is influencing the way we think about everything. An understanding that is breathing the spirit and mystery back into our perception of reality. Both of these worldviews embrace the concept of life existing within a living system, replacing the mechanical non-living view of reality.

The purpose of this part of the journey is to build a bridge between these two diverging worldviews of knowledge to understand where the theories are united. Both of these worldviews are valuable to the exploration of intuition, or the mysterious unseen aspect of human consciousness and intelligence.

Similar to my experience and the intuitions of my family members the ancient people knew without needing to know or explain how they knew. Intuitive intelligence was just a part of everyday existence and was accepted. With Western culture being more left brain and intellectual we require greater factual evidence before coming to a place of acceptance and understanding.

With this bridge of shared understanding, I intend to raise intuitively derived knowledge to a higher level of respectability within our social systems as a viable pathway to knowing and awakening our genius.

Mysticism meets Science

For thousands of years, medicine men/women, mystics and spiritual leaders have talked about the 'energy' surrounding living things. Because this had never been 'proven' scientifically it was discounted by the rational mind. Now of course it has been 'proven', so it is being accepted. Initially it was intuitive.

Intuition is the foundation of creativity when it is in concert with a strong rational thought process. Each of us need to encourage both processes.

All of the leading people in this new age of restructuring strongly believe in the value of our intuition as a tool for creativity and innovation.

Moore, L.
Getting Past the Rapids: Voyageur Lessons Learned

Ancient Wisdom
Indigenous Ways of Knowing

Shamanism is an ancient tradition that appears in cultures throughout the world. In indigenous societies, the primary keeper of ancient wisdom is the shaman. According to the Tungus of Siberia, the root meaning of shaman is "to know." This same individual may also be referred to in the community as a healer, wizard, seer, sorcerer or sage. The shaman is considered to be an explorer of human consciousness in which they enter through altered states or trance, to connect with both inner and outer sources of wisdom.

For indigenous people the earth is their Mother and she is a living breathing being and the source of life. Looking through this lens the whole world is ablaze with energy—a vibration that is flowing, ebbing and pulsating. All forms on earth and in the universe are perceived as interconnected, with a universal life force flowing through everything that we can see and everything that we cannot see. In this worldview energy is matter, and matter is spirit. One of the common hallmarks of a genuine mystical experience is a sense of unity in which all boundaries between the self and the other dissolve.

Although Indigenous peoples have been deeply traumatized by the legacy of Residential Schools, the Indian

Act, the confinement to reservations, the loss of spiritual traditions and livelihood they remain culturally connected to both the heart and spirit in ways that our Western society has difficulty perceiving and understanding. Indigenous beliefs encourage a way of being where intuition, dreams and insights from the natural world are accepted as messages from the invisible world of spirit, or supernatural to the world of physical reality. As in my vision, they also believe that we walk in this world with the support and guidance of our ancestors, our Grandmothers and our Grandfathers.

In the Greater Victoria School District children of First Nations descent are taught that the spiritual dimension of human development has four related capacities. The capacity to have and to respond to dreams, visions, ideals and spiritual teachings. The capacity to accept these as a reflection of our unknown or unrealized potential and the capacity to express these using symbols in speech, art or mathematics. Along with the capacity to use this symbolic expression towards action directed at making intuitions or nudging of the spirit a reality. In this worldview children are nurtured and taught principles of personal leadership that make them more open and receptive to intuitive intelligence. Those individuals with a heightened sensitivity are respected spiritual leaders, who often become the shamans providing guidance to their community though their communion and understanding of the spirit world.

Mental Health or Spiritual Emergence?

Early on in an individual's life, tribal members may observe, what the Western world would consider a psychotic episode, as a sign of a person needing healing or in the early stages of a spiritual emergence. It was a sign to begin initiation and training into the way of the shaman. In Western culture we often diagnose similar behaviors as neurosis or psychosis which demonstrates the differences in cultural perceptions or the mental models shaping our reality.

In most wisdom cultures, initiation rites included long periods of silence and solitude, where a form of meditation, mantra and prayer is a pre-requisite for obtaining mental clarity and enlightenment. The initiation process includes matching the intuitive individual with an Elder or mentor who has already travelled through the path and can therefore act as a guide to fully awaken the genius of the spirit. In this way, intuitive gifts can be nurtured in a safe and supportive environment. In the indigenous community there are rites of passage and years of training that support a gifted individual, or shaman along their evolutionary path. Individual gifts are recognized early and developed to their full potential in a supportive environment to provide sacred guidance to the community in resolving conflict, healing and decision-making.

Indigenous cultures throughout the planet demonstrate ways of being and knowing that nurture intuitive intelligence. With their belief in the oneness of the universe and inherent respect for nature it provides a model for sustaining life on Mother Earth.

A Shaman's World

Shaman's worlds and levels are more than interconnected; they are believed to interact with one another. Shamans believe that these interactions can be perceived and affected with one another. Shaman's believe that these interactions can be perceived and affected by one who knows how to do so and that the Shaman, like the spider at the center of a cosmic web, can feel and influence distant realms.

Walsh, R.
The Spirit of Shamanism

Quantum Physics

Quantum imagery challenges so many of our basic assumptions, including our understanding of relationship, connectedness, prediction and control. It may also be true that quantum phenomena apply to us larger sized objects, literally more than we thought. Our brain cells "are sensitive enough to register the absorption of a single photon . . . and thus sensitive enough to be influenced by a whole panoply of odd, quantum behavior"

Zohar, as cited in Margaret Wheatley
Leadership and the New Science:
Discovering Order in a Chaotic World

New Science
Weaving Spirit Back into Matter

New Science is opening us up to a new way of seeing that is helping to put the spirit and mystery back into our perceptions of life. Humanity is in the midst of transitioning between two major world paradigms; Newtonian Science and New Science and our world as we have known it is changing at a very rapid pace.

I first wrote this section in 2004 while conducting research for my thesis on "Intuition and Leadership: The Art of Wise Decision-Making." Revisiting this field of study, nine years later I am astonished by yet another paradigm shift through String Theory. A proposed theory of everything which is blurring the lines between divinity and science.

To start, we will explore the basics of quantum theory as understood through my research in 2004 followed by an extremely simplified version of String Theory. A wealth of videos and literature can be found on the internet for those wishing a deeper understanding.

Quantum Physics

The quantum world is mysterious, even to scientists and since research first began in the early nineteen hundreds it has slowly been influencing the Western worldview of reality. For example, studies conducted on electrons can result in them appearing as waves or as particles depending upon the intention of the observer and the design of the experiment. This finding demonstrates that other forces such as consciousness or intention have the ability to influence the outcome of reality.

This single finding has had implications upon many other areas of scientific research including matter, electromagnetic energy, light and sound. To better understand the paradoxical behavior of the quantum world, light is a vibration in the electromagnetic field and matter is that which can absorb light . . . light is that which can move freely between particles of matter" (Sheldrake & Fox, 1996, p.136). The quantum world is therefore, an unseen dance between matter, energy, light and sound.

Fields

Nature is organized by fields and fields are states of energy spread out over space. Unlike physical objects, different fields can occupy the same space at the same time and can interpenetrate each other. According to Bohm (1980), a theorist on Implicate Order, these energies are continually enfolding information concerning the entire universe of matter into each region of space. In a social sense, people become fields of energy that interpenetrate with the fields of others which collectively creates organized systems such as families, communities and culture. These fields of energy contain information, information that can be interpreted by a person sensitive to energy fields.

Patterns of Energy

Electromagnetic radiation is energy, and information in this sense becomes understood as patterns of energy. A radio is the metaphor most commonly used to describe this concept but today we could imagine our intuition as operating in a similar fashion to a cell phone, or our WiFi devices. By visualizing how we can tune into a frequency and listen to information being sent from other places in the world, we can begin to understand the capacity of the intuitive person to read electromagnetic patterns of energy.

The space between the sender and the receiver appears empty, but in actuality, it is full of information that can only be translated by tuning into the correct frequency. The gift of the intuitive person is their ability to tune into this frequency where they can interpret and translate the information which is received in a variety of formats such as dreams or visions.

Intuition is having the ability to see and feel the big picture or the whole system, while mysteriously tapping into unseen information contained within the energy of a system. According to quantum physics this energy is continuously flowing within and throughout all systems, from the smallest unit of matter to the largest.

This is a brief snapshot of scientific discoveries in the quantum physics a decade ago. Next we will explore the research and proposed theories that are shaping our worldview today.

String Theory

The Proposed Theory of Everything

As demonstrated through my earlier storytelling, I am not a scientist, nor do I have a left brained mathematical mind that operates through logic and facts. I am an artist, writer, visionary and intuitive so I will do my best in the language of symbols, visualizations and metaphors to explain this proposed theory within my understanding. String Theory is the latest in science and the discoveries are mind blowing, earth shattering and breathtaking in their complexity, beauty and harmony.

Dimensions of Realty

- The single universe that we can touch in the physical reality is being replaced by the concept of multi-universes.
- Our understanding of a 3 dimensional world is now believed to have 11 dimensions; with 10 dimensions in space and a single dimension in time.
- These dimensions can be thought of as individual soap bubbles that contain a separate reality within each bubble or dimension, resulting in the possibility of other universes occurring right beside, above or below us without our having any awareness of their existence.

The Microcosm and the Macrocosm

As a child, my daughter used to stare at small creatures like wood bugs and ants, butterflies and tadpoles and use her imagination to try and visualize their worlds as a way of shaping and forming her own sense of reality. It comes of no surprised to me that scientists today are using the worldview of bugs like ants to try and help the general population understand this emerging multidimensional view of reality.

An ant crawling up a tree trunk cannot be seen by me while sipping tea in a café across the street, although I can see the tree in the park through the front window. It is only when I go outside and walk over to the tree that I can see that the ant is there and crawling in and throughout the bark. Ants exist even though I cannot see them from far away, and access worlds I can only visualize through my imagination.

This same image holds true whether I am looking at the world of a bug or the stars in the night sky. What holds everything in existence in place is an invisible force, known as the web of life or the vibrating fabric of existence by shamans.

May the Force Be With You!

According to science there are 4 forces at work in the universe. These forces act like an invisible matrix, a spider's web or a field suspended throughout time and space. These 4 forces are gravity, electromagnetic forces and both weak and strong nuclear forces. Scientist ponder the existence of a 5th force and the possibility that this 5th force could be psychic phenomena or forms of telepathy.

From the perspective of a woman who lives with an intuitive view of reality there are a lot of problems with trying to prove this gift within the constructs of science as I understand it. Scientific theories must have the ability to be tested upon arriving at the same outcome each time in order to validate any theory as truth. If the test fails even once, the theory is deemed false and therefore, dismissed.

The major problem that I see with psychic phenomena being proven as a theory within this model is that it does not take into account the vast number of variables and factors at play when applying quantum science to people. To name just a few that come to mind are the various stages of human development, differences in age, gender, culture, health and well-being, the influence of belief systems, parenting, spiritual development and ability to interpret information by the receiver.

Also, what is the complexity of the problem? If you are Einstein then this is going to be a question of universal implications and may take a lifetime or two and a leap in human consciousness before an "Aha" moment is finally delivered and received.

Dark Matter

Most of the dimensions of space that exist cannot be seen. In fact, according to the chart below the majority is invisible to the naked eye, making other realities non-existent to the awareness of human beings. In truth this vast space is full, not empty as was once thought. If we imagine ourselves as the ant for a moment, our view of the space around us is limited to what we can see and touch through our senses.

Percentage	The Form of Our Universe
73 %	Dark Energy
23 %	Invisible Dark Matter
4 %	Stars
.03 %	Us & the Universe

String Theory

String Theory is believed to be the theory of everything embracing the microcosm and the macrocosm, and is comprised of particles that include atoms, electrons, neutrinos, protons and quarks.

Deep inside all particles is a vibrating string of energy, with each string vibrating at a different frequency that when heard together sounds similar to musical notes playing in a symphony. These strings can be visualized as tiny rubber bands floating in hyper-space interconnecting everything within each and all of the dimensions.

This is the Cosmic Music that Albert Einstein searched for his whole life.

Leading research into New Science is providing a whole new way of seeing reality, and it parallels the indigenous and shamanic understandings of a living interconnected universe. In both of these worlds, the universe is imagined as a living organism that displays a mysterious telepathy-type interconnectedness.

It is my belief that the information vibrating within these strings is woven throughout everything, and can be communicated in a language known by children, animals, sensitive's, indigenous peoples and understood intuitively by everyone to varying degrees.

String Theory in a Dream?

I was very close to my Grandfather, and when he passed away I kept having repeating dreams of this single strand of thread connecting me to him, that had become detached when he left his physical body. This thread was similar to a filament or strand on a spider's web and was still connected to my core but no longer connected to the physical being of my Grandfather. In my dreams, I could see this thread floating loosely in the wind leaving me with the feeling of being off balance. During my grieving process I began searching to reconnect this loose thread to some other physical object or person in order to stabilize my presence once again in the living world.

I believe these dreams were showing me just how deeply we are all invisibly connected to one another. I shared this story with the Hospice Counsellor whom I was receiving grief counselling from and she confirmed that my experience was commonly shared by others going through the loss of a loved one.

Institute for the Noetic Sciences

"The word "noetic" comes from the Greek word nous . . . and refers to an 'inner knowing' a kind of intuitive consciousness—direct and immediate access to knowledge beyond what is available to our normal senses and the power of reason.

Noetic sciences are explorations into the nature and potentials of consciousness using multiple ways of knowing—including intuition, feeling, reason, and the senses. Noetic sciences explore the 'inner cosmos' of the mind (consciousness, soul, spirit) and how it relates to the 'outer cosmos' of the physical world.

The goal of this work is to support individuals in the transformation of their own consciousness (developing their innate human potentials and creative capacities) as a foundation for collective transformation toward a global wisdom society."

The Institute for Noetic Sciences
http://noetic.org/

Intuition
Another Way of Knowing

Human Development & Resonance

One respondent described intuition in terms of levels of human development, discussing the resonance of historical figures like Christ and Mohammad. The discussion surrounded the gift of insight that so many figures throughout history had, and their ability to resonate so powerfully throughout time. Resonate powerfully enough for people to kill them and yet their knowledge continued to resonate on for many thousands of years into the future. This led them to believe that these leaders probably had some extra-ordinary intuition, some extraordinary insight that probably came to them from somewhere between the intellect and pure emotion.

That was intuition.

Anonymous

Intuition
Another Way of Knowing

My lifelong curiosity about the mystery of intuition led me to conduct a research project during my graduate studies dedicated solely to intuition and leadership. It was a fascinating exploration and the following are some of the insightful comments people used to describe their intuitive process.

- A sixth sense, using another sense . . . a feeling
- GPS or Guidance System
- Energizing—A synchronistic flow

Intuition Defined

Intuition: the ability to know

Clairsentience: the ability to sense spirit

Clairvoyance: the ability to see spirit

Clairaudience: the ability to hear spirit

Spiritual Medium: people who are able to communicate to those on the other side: in tune with the spirit world

Communication: Inspirational speaking, inspirational writing,

Spiritual Healing: a channel for divine healing

Telepathy: communication between one person and another without physical contact, transference of information

All life is spirit encased in matter. This spirit, an unseen force or a psychic energy creates the interconnection.

- Wisdom is the connection between the head and the heart . . . a connection between the known and the unknown. A connection between the head and heart is the concept that was most frequently discussed during the conversations and is an idea conveyed by indigenous peoples.
- Intuition is sight . . . you can see ahead of time what is going to happen
- Feels emotional
- Intuition is a variety of things but one of the more important things is how I am feeling tells me that in the context of everything that I know about the issue that I made the right decision. If I do not have that feeling then I need to do more work.
- It is a kind of synthesis of the various things. It is like the gut feel type of intuition which if I had to try and define it is a kind of synthesis of the various things I know. Signals are made available to my consciousness.
- I recall a gut feeling. Other data may be pointing in one direction but my gut feel is point me in another direction. I think that I have to say that for me it is the gut. It is the moment that you converge something known with something unknown.

The interviews I conducted revealed diverse personal definitions of intuition however, there were common threads between the literature, my personal experiences and the definitions obtained through my conversations.

Both the literature and the participants described intuition as a synthesis of knowledge and experience, or a connection between the known (consciousness) and the unknown (subconscious). The word "synthesis" is the most commonly used word to describe intuition. Synthesis of the mind and the soul and they collaborate to expand our awareness.

Other key words used by the research participants included a gut feeling, convergence and establishing connections between opposing modes of knowing such as the intellect and pure emotion. A review of literature identified the terms non-linear intelligence, divine intelligence, immediate cognition and natural knowing.

My personal experiences as the researcher and a participant further support the ideas shared by participants and in my review of literature. While conducting most of the interviews I found myself doodling the symbol of a cross with a circle around the center point (convergence) in the margins of my notes. This symbol would flash into my mind's eye during conversations and was triggered by the spoken words. I interpreted the center of the cross to symbolize the place of transcendence or synthesis between two complementary opposites such as: known and unknown; head and heart; right and left brain and masculine and feminine to name a few.

I am offering my personal experience as an example of an intuitively derived definition. Unlike the participants my definition arose through symbols that flashed in my mind which I then drew on paper, allowing me to interpret the meaning of that symbol as it reflected back into my consciousness. My intuitive process included imagery, drawing and looking for patterns as a process for interpreting and meaning making.

"Wisdom is a connection between the head and the heart . . . I believe it is a whole body as connected to life feeling."

Kundalini Yoga

Yoga, meditation and Buddhism have been integral aspects of my personal life over the past fifteen years. I have been particularly drawn to Kundalini Yoga, which is a practice of opening your heart and attuning to your true nature through the unfolding of your Soul. All yoga aims to increase the relationship between individual consciousness and the Infinite or Universal consciousness.

The style of kundalini that I practice was brought to the west in the late sixties by Yogi Bhajan a leader, master and visionary who was following his destiny. Yogi Bhajan brought these teachings to the west in preparation for the Aquarian Age. The grand transition projected for 2012, as foretold in the prophecies of wisdom traditions throughout the globe. The Aquarian Age is said to be a time of truth and beliefs based upon knowledge. It is a transition that will unfold the maturity within human beings, releasing humanity from the relentless competition, information overload and ecological challenges. It is the end of the world as we think of the world, through the dissolving of old structures, ways of being, where the unconscious becomes conscious. Collectively opening up space for the unleashing of the expansiveness of hearts and our Creative Spirit.

During this time period, individuals will need to do the work necessary to clear out the old patterns stored in our subconscious mind. Through activities such as meditation, silence, stillness, breath and kriyas you become more aware of your negative habits, cycles and repeating mental and emotional patterns. The goal of this work and awareness is to continually polish the diamond within your mind. These patterns become established frequencies and projections that radiate out from us into the consciousness of the world.

The goal of yoga is to awaken the Self that is the Soul through union. Self-realization in conscious relationship to the total universal awareness can also be thought of as intuition. The answers you need can be found within. The chant *"Ong Namo Guru Dev Namo"* is sang at the beginning of every kundalini yoga practice, and translates into the idea that, *"I bow to divine wisdom, the divine teacher within."* Your body is the temple of wisdom and your spirit is the flow of universal cosmic energy. Intuition is your ability to act in synchronicity with this flow of the universal cosmic energy. A transcendental place where you experience the Oneness and Unity of all things. In my experience kundalini yoga has been a powerful tool for awakening that increases your sensitivity, radiance and intuition.

The Language of the Soul

Intuition communicates to everyone in a language that is as unique as each person. Some people experience intuition as a feeling, other people hear a voice, or have a dream or experience a clear vision. Still others may feel a sudden increase in energy, make a link while speaking to a stranger, have an insightful dream or an experience of synchronicity. A challenge for everyone is interpreting intuitive information as it arrives in such diverse forms.

According to Shakti Gawain (2000), author of numerous books on developing intuition, the information received doesn't necessarily make logical sense. Sometimes a period of time is required to make the links between the problem and the insight. Another challenge is distinguishing your intuitive voice from the other voices within yourself (Gawain, 2000; Bodine, 2001). Each person is complex and individuals embody a life time of experiences to decode in a myriad of different voices, feelings, beliefs and values. The best way to learn to understand the language of intuition is to practice reflective exercises that are designed to enhance self-awareness and increase self-knowledge.

Connecting the Known & the Unknown

You find yourself making associations that are not immediately self-evident. Sometimes it can feel very strange because it can trigger associations that really may not have anything to do with the substance of what someone said. I read a lot and sometimes when I am reading and all of the sudden, "Boom!" It will trigger an association that has nothing to do with what I am reading, but it automatically connects everything and when this happens there is a tremendous sense of energy. It is an energizing experience! At the same time it is nervous energy that I do not want to slip away. I do not want to lose that feeling of synchronicity. I may not have that insight for very long. I have got to write it down.

It is that sense of knowing. It comes about by a connection between the known and the unknown, the familiar and the unfamiliar. You can see it and know it and capture it. Such an emotional and powerful sensation.

Anonymous

The Wedding of Physics & Consciousness

David Bohm's work on non-locality and his wedding of physics and consciousness have caused some para-psychologists to look to his theory for an explanation of such phenomena as telepathy, precognition and psycho-kinesis.

In Implicate Order, the totality of existence is enfolded within each fragment of space and time—whether it be a single object, thought or event. Thus everything in the universe affects everything else because they are all part of the same unbroken whole.

Joseph Jaworski
Synchronicity: The Inner Path of Leadership

Intuitive
Leadership

Intuitive Leadership

Our global society is changing at a rapid pace and new knowledge is constantly streaming forth into our consciousness presenting new challenges. Enfolding this information into our awareness while exploring and collaborating on innovative ideas and new models of living is essential at this time in our evolution.

Intuitive leadership is the idea that we are all leaders who create change inspired by our own dreams and intuitions and is a path towards personal mastery. It is empowered living through being at one with your divine essential Self and the Universe.

Leaders are those individuals who understood the situation they found themselves living in, and made a conscious decision to courageously step forward to voice their dreams and become a part of the change they desired to see. A few of the leaders known in more recent times include: Vandana Shiva, Rosa Parks, Rigoberta Menchu, Nelson Mandela, His Holiness The Dalai Lama, Mahatma Gandhi and Martin Luther King. These men and women all faced difficult challenges which they overcame (or are working to overcome) through a power based upon a commitment to the cause, and peaceful actions. The essence of their leadership style and influence is rooted in concepts traditionally linked to the hippy movement of the 1960's but in truth the most effective leaders throughout history have called upon the energy of peace and love. We are all leaders in our own worlds, no matter the size.

A leader is one who has a dream or a vision, and the creative ability to manifest their dreams into reality. The scope of our dreams and our visions is as vast and diverse as life itself. This may be a dream for your children or your family, a dream for yourself, or your profession, or you may care deeply about a threatened species or an area of wilderness. You may dream of planting a garden to grow organic food that your children can gather for dinner, or have a dream to improve the wellness of your community or you may have a dream with global reaches such as clean air to breathe. All dreams are equally valuable.

Your dreams and your intuitions are your guide to awakening.

Intuitive leadership is a tool for holistic thinking and empowered living. Every human being has an internal guidance or navigational system living inside them. Both intuition and leadership require self-awareness and self-knowledge which is key to the development of this gift. Intuitive leadership respects and integrates the analytical thinking of the left brain and the creative feminine of the right brain, opening up the doorway to other ways of knowing, being and doing.

Intuitive leadership is a path towards personal mastery as guided by another way of knowing. It is the idea that we are all leaders in our own life, leaders who have the ability to transform dreams into reality as inspired by our intuitions.

Self-Awareness & Self-Knowledge

Both leadership and intuition require high levels of self-awareness and self-knowledge which is the awareness of your authentic self. There are many ancient wisdom quotes, but perhaps one of the most famous is from the bible, "Know Thy Self." The challenge to authenticity requires a courageous heart and a powerful mind to grow beyond the confines of our known reality and to step outside of our familiar box. Self-awareness and self-knowledge are integral to spiritual practices and wisdom cultures throughout the world.

In yoga, the Ego is the identification with a false Self, and much of the practice of yoga is to help us uncover the many illusions we hold about reality. A foundational principle is that we are born in perfection, and that our work is to clean and polish the brilliant gem that lies within, allowing more of our inner light to radiate out. Regular practice of yoga supports students to live fully present in each moment, bringing the light of our consciousness into our day to day experiences for reflection and transformation. Through the practice of presence we are slowly restored back to our true nature; embodying more self-aware awareness and self-knowledge.

According to psychologists, only 5% of our reality is conscious to us, with the other 95% embedded deep within our unconscious mind. This 95% is very powerful and influences how we operate in our day to day lives. An iceberg is the easiest image to visualize to understand how the unconscious operates in your life. Only a very small portion the iceberg is visible to the naked eye, with the remaining and much larger portion sitting under water and therefore, unseen by the naked eye. This portion of the iceberg that is underwater and invisible to us, has tremendous power, enough power to sink a famous ship like the Titanic. Our unconscious mind acts in a very similar way.

Stored deep in the unconscious mind are memories we may prefer not to remember, along with assumptions and beliefs that direct our thoughts, words, and actions. Much of what is stored in the unconscious may not even be true when recovered, and reflected upon. If this information is left stored in the unconscious, these false ideas become the false self, the shadow, or the ego. Bringing the information to light can be thought of as polishing the diamond of your soul, and accomplished through a variety of techniques including: daily journaling, walking in nature, reflection, meditation, yoga, breath work, dance, conversation and silence.

Consciousness = 5 %	Unconsciousness = 95 %

In Hinduism, wisdom is knowing oneself as the truth and as an expression of the entire Creation. It is essential therefore, to heal, clear away and transform the false beliefs and the lies in our mind that we unconsciously tell ourselves about the nature of reality. Otherwise, we will hear the voice of another influential person in our life like our mother or father instead of our intuitive intelligence.

The Road to Discovery

The intellect has little to do on the road to discovery.

There comes a leap in consciousness, call it intuition or what you will, and the solution comes to you and you don't know how or why . . .

Albert Einstein

The Healing Journey

For the most part we have been conditioned into being. As a little child this conditioning starts with our parents and is later followed by the layers upon layers added on by our family, environment and social systems. In the larger context, history, science and patriarchy have also influenced our beliefs, perceptions and our values.

In more recent times, television and media has played a huge role in shaping our perceptions, beliefs and values regarding who we should be and what the world should look like. Generations of people have now been informed by media what to buy, how to live and what is important without stopping to reflect upon the information through the critical lens of their own personal truth.

Through the many layers of conditioning we begin losing touch with our own source of inner truth, and become disconnected from our intuition, our sacred source of knowing. In the indigenous worldview there is no separation between spirit and matter or between the social and environmental elements that create the web of life. Indigenous cultures demonstrate a way of being that listens to the voice of the human soul, the heartbeat of Mother Nature and the whispers from the Great Spirit. Our true nature in conscious relationship with the natural world. This is the authentic voice of our dreams, our feelings and intuitions. A voice of wisdom that can only become known when we believe that the world outside of ourselves is in direct communication with the world within.

Healing the separation involves excavating the beliefs and memories we have stored deep within our unconscious. Blocked memories that often separate us from the unified field of our true nature. These archived voices blur the purity of the inner voice of intuition and wall us off of from direct access to our authentic voice. The process of self-discovery leading to self-awareness and self-knowledge is the path of leadership and sometimes called shadow work.

The Shadow
Discovering Your Authentic Self

Children are naturally intuitive. They do not think, they just know. Nor do they analyze the truth of their knowledge as it is integral to their very being and to their existence. There are no separations within the child Self. My grandson demonstrated this through his absolute confidence in "knowing" that his Mama was coming despite what I said to the contrary. He just knew.

We are born in perfection, fully embodying the truth of our Authentic Self and connected to a divine source of intelligence and wisdom. As little children we are full of innocence, purity and joy as we tumble about in delightful discovery of the world around us.

Our Shadow begins to develop right here in our innocence, purity and joyfulness. It is made up of all the hurts from the voices that ridiculed, criticized or shamed us for simply being our true self. Even though we are born in divine perfection we are taught through social conditioning that who we are is not good enough and must be changed. Our suffering develops through our striving to become perfect, although were born through our Mothers as perfection.

We learn to feel afraid of fully expressing our true nature, and very early start silencing parts of our essential self in order to find acceptance. As little children we learn the art of pretending and begin cutting off our feelings and repressing the natural flow of life. We have no choice. Fitting in and belonging is critical to our survival, but fitting in also means that parts of our true self must separate and go into hiding. Over time we keep hiding more and more of the hurt and shamed parts of our self until we have created a false self that we hope, is finally acceptable to society.

By the time we reach our adult life the Shadow has taken on a life of its own which can be observed through destructive patterns of behavior and found in our negative emotions and projections. The stories we gathered up from the voices of the past often haunt us without having any consciousness of their presence and influence in our life.

The disowned and now hidden parts of our true Self are known by many names besides the Shadow, including: the dark side, our demons, the hungry ghost, lost child or lost soul. Eckhart Tolle in his popular books refers to this indwelling energy as the pain body. Whatever name it is called, it is a place of deep suffering that requires the salve of love, kindness and acceptance to begin healing and bringing us back into wholeness.

The patterns of our being become repetitive, with earlier traumas repeating their cycles of behavior throughout our life and often becoming embedded in intergenerational patterns of behavior. These are the places in our Soul where we have lost conscious contact and communion with our heart and our feelings. In order to dissolve our Shadow we must make friends with it when we feel these patterns and uncomfortable energies arise within us. The fearful, hurt and discarded parts of our Self are only asking to be seen, felt, heard and healed. When triggered, embrace the Shadow by calling the energy out into the light where it can be embraced for helping us overcome past challenges. As we gather up separated parts of our self we start feeling more of our essential nature and step further along the path back home, to our Authentic Self.

Shadow work is messy and uncomfortable. It takes a courageous heart to allow painful memories to re-surface and to consciously feel those unwanted and often negatively charged feelings we have blocked off. There are many techniques to support healing the Shadow such as self-reflection, journaling, dance, therapy, art, yoga, music, meditation and conversation. Debbie Ford is perhaps one of the best known educators on healing the Shadow and has written numerous books on the subject that can be used as a resource.

As the channel becomes clearer, cleaner and less cluttered by the voices of the past, you move closer to your heart and your true nature. Your childlike sense of wonder returns, you feel more joy as you become more intimately connected to the flow of information received from your intuitive intelligence. This is the "returning home to your heart" that the Grandmothers were referring to in the vision. Living life from a place of authenticity is living a life empowered by your own sacred communion with the mystery.

Like the salmon returning home from the sea, we are often going against the established structures and their energetic currents when on the healing journey. Therefore, it can get very tiring as there are many high waterfalls to jump over on the way back home. As a little girl growing up in an alcoholic family I know. There have been times along my own healing journey that I just didn't think I had the energy or the courage to face and transcend yet another memory of hurt, a false belief or a place of separation, but I did, and I still do . . . as it is a lifelong process of the reconnecting the human spirit.

Focused Attention +
Abandonment = Intuitive Insight

The most characteristic circumstances of an intuition are a period of intense work on a problem accompanied by a desire for its solution, abandonment of the work perhaps with attention to something else then the appearance of the idea with dramatic suddenness and often a sense of certainty.

A feeling of exhilaration!

By Jeremy Narby
The Cosmic Serpent

Accessing Your Inner Guru

Intuitive Guidance & Decision-Making

The following steps provide a framework for accessing your inner Guru, Genius or Genie by tapping into your intuitive intelligence for guidance, problem-solving and decision-making. This is a general framework because intuition is a process that is random, non-linear, non-logical and circular so it becomes a co-creative dance between yourself and the universe.

I was born into a family where my Elders shared their dreams, insights and voices that provided warnings that kept loved ones safe, or fore told events in a future time. My daughter, grandson and Elders knew without knowing how they knew. The intuitive voice was common language to my young ears which likely made me more curious and open to listening to this voice as spoken through my daughter and my grandson.

I believe intuition is a gift that we are all born with in varying degrees and it is a source of internal intelligence that can slowly slip away over time. As a result, activating your intuition and understanding the communication may take time and conscious effort.

The genius, Einstein imagined Mother Nature and the Universe as a wonderful mystery that he was a participant in. A large part of Einstein's brilliance was in his openness to new insights and ideas in order to shed light on old problems and old ways of thinking. He loved to dream and openly paid tribute to his intuition as being the source of his genius; the use of both his logical and intuitive intelligence as it manifested through him.

The gift of intuition is the creative whisper from the Universe to you that is available for guidance and encouragement as you to reach for your full potential in all areas of your life.

Intuitive Guidance

Step	Action	Form
1.	**Believe**	Believe that you exist in an interconnected & participatory Universe that is responsive to your needs & wishes.
2.	**Reflect & Research**	Thoroughly understand the nature of the problem or the situation you wish to receive guidance on.
3.	**Frame the question in clear and positive language**	Write the question down choosing positive words and in a form that clearly articulates what you wish for, want to know or understand. Speak the question out loud and silently in your mind.
4.	**Ask**	Request support & guidance from the Universe in resolving the issue, question or desire.
5.	**Silence**	• Pray • Meditate • Walk in Nature
6.	**Let Go!**	Now that you know what you wish for guidance on—let it go and allow the Universe to respond in its own time and in its own way. • *dance, garden, play, cook, create, clean, build . . .*

7.	Be Open to Receive	The Universe responds in a language and form that is unique to you
8.	Listen to Messages from both Inner & Outer Worlds	Be Present: The Universe is responding. Listen careful as your answer may come in a variety of forms including: • Through Your Dreams • Through another person • Creative Insight • A Sign • A Symbol or Vision • A Feeling • A Pattern Recognition • A Solid Sense of Knowing • A Nudging to go somewhere, do something, see someone or read an article etc.
9.	Interpret the Response	Consciously interpret the language of your soul. Messages may be delivered in fragments or in symbols. Sometimes, the response received does not appear directly connected to the question, wish or prayer. Guidance from your intuitive intelligence provides answers in the highest form and are relevant to the present moment. Sometimes the bigger picture that is unfolding is not within our immediate view, but is revealed and understood in a later time.
10.	Action	Decide how you wish to respond based upon the guidance received through your intuitive intelligence. Courageous action may be required but ultimately, all decisions are based entirely upon individual free will.

Stillness Speaks

Is it not wisdom that humanity needs most at this time?

But what is wisdom and where is it to be found? Wisdom comes with the ability to be still. Just look and just listen. No more is needed. Being still, looking and listening activates that non-conceptual intelligence within you. Let stillness direct your words and actions.

Is stillness just the absence of noise and content? No, it is intelligence itself—the underlying consciousness out of which every form is born. And how could that be separate from who you are.

It is the essence of the all the galaxies and blades of grass; of all the flowers, trees, birds and all of forms.

Eckhart Tolle

A New Dream
of Earth

A New Story

As he hurtled through space a thought occurred to him, perhaps reality is more complex, subtle, and inexorably mysterious than conventional science had led him to believe. Perhaps a deep understanding of consciousness (inner space) could lead to a new and expanded view of reality in which objective and subjective, outer and inner, are understood as equal aspects of the miracle and mystery of being.

"I realized that the story of ourselves as told by science—our cosmology, our religion—was incomplete and likely flawed. I recognized that the Newtonian idea of separate, independent, discreet things in the universe wasn't a fully accurate description.

What was needed was a new story of who we are and what we are capable of becoming."

Edgar Mitchell
Institute of the Noetic Sciences
Noetikos: inner/intuitive knowing
http://noetic.org

A New Dream of Earth

The Gift was inspired after receiving a vision from an ancient feminine presence that I intuited as *"The Grandmothers"* a vision given to me while I lay deep within the stillness of my own soul. It was the spring of 2010, and the year I turned fifty. I was already a Grandmother, but still learning how to enfold this new role into my being.

The Grandmothers of the Sea, the Land and the Sky communicated a need for a radical shift in human consciousness and behavior. A shift away from the love of power and towards the power of love. The wise creatures I met during the vision expressed their growing exhaustion as a result of the pollution and destructive patterns of behavior affecting all life on the planet. *"It is time"* they silently whispered. *"It is time to go home."* To the home within our heart, to the place of intuitive knowing, feeling and being. The ancient feminine presence guided me on the vision with the hopes that I would respond. It took three years. The first year I completely forgot about the vision. During the second year though, the vision kept returning to momentarily fill my consciousness, and a year later I blacked out. This was my wake up call to take action, and the words you are reading today are my response to the persistent nudging of spirit. The sharing of my story and my journey of discovery into another way of knowing.

To indigenous peoples, we live on Mother Earth. She is our home in the Universe and our health is intimately connected to her well-being. There is no separation. We are all intricately linked together in the rich tapestry of life. Everything connected by an invisible thread linking the One to the All. The famous shaman artist, Norval Morriseau painted an interconnected world filled with brilliant color, love and divine relationships. A Heaven on Earth that humanity could create if we visualized all the possibilities.

In reality though, the life we are painting on our planetary canvas more often resembles a war zone. Our home, which is considered alive and conscious by traditional peoples and by many scientists today is suffering and struggling to maintain balance. On top of this, the film industry is constantly streaming forth apocalyptic movies which give the illusion that reality is a nightmare and forecasting that life on the planet is going to end in destruction. The constant downloading of these negative images through television, technology and film is taking away all of our hope, along with the hopes for our children, our grandchildren and future generations. We have the power though to find the switch that turns off the illusionary nightmare, and begin filling the empty space with new dreams of life on Earth. Dreams that inspire our highest creative potential as human beings.

Coming Home

See the majesty of the powerful ocean with her pounding surf
And sparkling blue waters, the embryo of life
Gazing upwards towards the heavenly blue sky
Or the moon and stars as they shine in the twilight
Feeling our toes root into the soft soil of Mother Earth
Eyes soaking in the plant kingdom

With her radiant colors, exquisite beauty and rich diversity
Wondrous winged insects: butterflies, birds and bumble bees
Imagine the little boy who waddled through the forest
To lovingly hug a tree
Can you now see?
This is the Great Mystery
You are an Ancient Presence
Breath
Tuning inwards,
Listen to the drumming of your heart beat
See your words carried upon the wind, the water and landscape
Humanity is coming home to their Heart
To our home on Mother Earth
As she spins through the Universe
Living is proof of magic, mystery and miracles.

I was a little girl born into an environment rich in intuitive ways of knowing. The experience positioned me to be both comfortable and curious about other ways of knowing. I am not a medium, nor am I a channeler or a psychic. I am just an ordinary woman living in extraordinary times. I am highly intuitive and believe that intuition is a Universal Gift that we are all born with, but lose touch with over time in our striving to become what the world tells us we should be. Intuitive knowing is the gift we receive when we return home to our essential Self.

As Albert Einstein reminds us,

"The intuitive mind is a Sacred Gift and the rational mind a faithful servant. We have created a society that honours the servant and has forgotten the Gift."

This Gift is a jewel that lives within our hearts and can be polished to shine brightly and radiate upon our children, our families and our organizations leading us to our highest individual and collective potential.

Intuition is listening to the voice of wisdom that resides within your heart and soul. Leadership requires self-awareness and self-knowledge to influence positive change in the world with the radiance of your truth and authenticity. Intuitive leadership is a path towards personal mastery. It is empowered living through being at one with your divine essential Self and the Universe.

I hope that the Grandmother's vision as translated through my words inspires new dreams of possibility for humanity, our children and our planet. Dreams that only your heart knows.

Peace & Love

Patti

Hunches

Hunches his mother used to call them. The boy was beginning to understand that intuition is really a sudden immersion of the soul into the universal current of life, where the histories of all people are connected, and we are able to know everything, because it is all written there.

(Coelho, 1998, p.74)

"Touch the Earth Gently"

Professional photograph by Jenna LeFebvre

Nixon Euchere
4 years old

Acknowledgements

This book would not have been written without the support of my brother Bill & his wife Jennifer. It was only during the writing of this book that I reconnected with my youngest brother after a ten year separation, and had the honour of meeting his beautiful wife and two daughters Kiley and Teagan. I am grateful for their heartfelt support over the course this project. To Shawn and Thomas for their interest in their history, and in the art of writing. To my Mother, Joan Birch, who lived her life with a courageous heart, and told me from the time I was a little girl that I needed to write because I had the gift.

I send my heartfelt thanks Vivek Voora, who for the past decade has supported, challenged and inspired me to grow and continually evolve as a woman. It was this beautiful and transcendental man who first sent me the writings from Dr. Clarissa Pinkola Estes on the Wild Woman Archetype. Fairy tale stories of the visionary abilities of women, and the intuitive and ageless knowing that comes from truly living from your instincts. These ideas spoke to my soul about loving and living wild and free, especially having spent most of my life on the wild westcoast of British Columbia.

To my girlfriend, Debbie Janes who is a woman living out her wildest dreams and who demonstrated true friendship by lending me her hand, heart and home when needed. Sending gratitude to Catherine for her beautiful writing space last winter and for our shared commitment to environmental education. To the beautiful and creative Jade deTrey for your dance and for shining your light and love. Hugs to Sheron Jutilla for the same, for shining your original brilliance and light in my world and allowing me to do the same. Namaste to my yoga friends and teachers throughout North America who have helped me to heal and bring balance to my body, my mind and Spirit. A special thanks to yoginis and teachers at the Yandara Yoga Institute in Mexico, where the Grandmother's came through in the vision that became the inspiration for this book on the New Dream.

To my mentors and colleagues in graduate school I thank you all. It was while at Royal Roads University that I first began transforming my beliefs about the gift of intuition. With the support of my Faculty Advisors, Mel McLeod who became my intuitive mentor, and Cathy MacKenzie who helped me translate my experience and knowledge into the written word. A special thanks to the creative brilliance of Greg Thorne of Thorne Creative who took my artwork and designed a cover I love.

To both my grandchildren, Nixon and Arianna. Your innocence and overflowing joy and enthusiasm for life fills my heart with unimaginable joy. A big thanks to their father, Nick, for giving his children the protection and support they need to just be themselves.

To my beautiful daughter Sascha Rose . . . you're my gift from the Creator. I thank you for everything: for your pure heart, your courage, compassion, creativity and for your instinctual mothering. As our favorite childhood storybook says, "I'll love you, forever and always."

References

Abram, David (2010). Becoming Animal: An Earthly Cosmology. NY, Pantheon Books (Division of Random House of Canada)

Anderson, J.A. (1999). Intuition in Managers: Are Intuitive Managers More Effective? Journal of Managerial Psychology

Ardagh, Arjuna (2005). The Translucent Revolution: How People just like you are Waking Up and Changing the World. Novato, CA: New World Library

Arrien, A. Ph.D (1993). The Four Fold Way: Walking the Paths of the Warrior, Teacher, Healer & Visionary. NY: HarperCollins Publishers.

Askim, R.E. (2002). Learning Circle Basics. http://www.magma.ca/-raksim/learning_circle.htm

Baldwin, C. (1998). Calling the Circle: The First and Future Cuture. Toronto, ON; Bantum Books

Baldwin, C. & Linnea, A. (1999). PeerSpirit Council Management, in business, corporations and organizations, Langley, BC: PeerSpirit.

Bodine, E. (2001). A Still Small Voice: A Psychic's Guide to Awakening Intuition. Novato, CA: New World Library.

Bohm, D. (1980). Wholeness and the Implicate Order. New York: Routledge

Bolte Taylor, J., Dr., (2008). Jill Bolte Taylor's Stroke of Insight. TEDXTalk, http://www.youtube.com/watch?v=UyyjU8fzEYU

Braden, G. (2007). The Divine Matrix: Bridging Time, Space, Miracles and Belief. NY, Hay House

Bryan, M., Cameron, J. & Allen, C. (1998). The Artists Way at Work: Riding the Dragon. New York: William Morrow and Company.

Capra, F. (1983). The Tao of Physics: An Exploration of the Parallels between Modern Physics and Easter Mysticism. Oxford: University Press

Chopra, D. & Mlodinow, L. (2012). War of Worldviews: Where Science and Spirituality Meet—and Do Not. N.Y., Three Rivers Press, a Division of Random House, Inc.

Chopra, D. & Ford, D. & Williamson, M. (2010). The Shadow Effect: Illuminating the Hidden Power of Your True Self. N.Y., HaperCollins

Chopra, D., M.D. & Tanzi, R., Ph.D. (2012). Super Brain: Unleashing the Explosive Power of Your Mind to Maximize Health, Happiness and Spiritual Well-Being. N.Y., Random House Inc.

Coelho, P. (1998). The Alchemist. New York: Harper Collins.

Cooperrider, D. (2003). Appreciative Inquiry. The Quote Center. http://www.appreciative-inquiry.org/AI-Quotes.htm

Cooperrider, D. & Srivastva, S. (1987). Appreciative Inquiry in Organizational Life. http://www.appreciative-inquiry.org/AI-Life-part2.htm

Drury, N. (1991). The Elements of Shamanism. Rockport, MA: Element, Inc.

Estes, C.P. Ph.D. (1997) Women Who Run With the Wolves: Myths and Stories of the Wild Woman Archetype. U.S.A., Random House, Inc.

Gawain, S. (2000). Developing Intuition: Practical Guidance for Daily Life. Novato, CA: Nataraj Publishing.

Golman, D. (2003). Destructive Emotions: How Can we Overcome Them? A Scientific Dialogue with the Dalhi Lama, NY: Bantum Books

Guiness, O.M. (2002). Systems Thinking. Course LT504. Victoria, BC: Royal Roads University

Greater Victoria School District, First Nations Education Division. (1996). First Nations Young People: Becoming Healthy Leaders for Today and Tomorrow. (Available through First Nations Education Division, 923 Topaz Avenue, Victoria, BC V8T 2M2)

Greene, B. (2005). Making Sense of String Theory, TEDXTalk http://www.ted.com/talks/brian_greene_on_string_theory.html

Hanh, T.N. (2007). The Art of Power. N.Y., HarperCollins

Harbisson, N. (2012). I Listen to Color, TEDXTalk, YouTube http://www.youtube.com/watch?v=ygRNoieAnzl

Hiley, B.J. & Peat, D.F. (1987). Quantum Implications: Essays in Honour of David Bohm. New York: Routledge & Kegan Paul.

Hollyhock (2004). 2004 Programs Holidays Conferences. (Available at P.O. Box 127, Manson's Landing, Cortez Island, BC V0P 1K0).

Institute of Noetic Sciences. (2003). What is Noetic? www.noetic.org/ions/new.html

Interpretive Report: Myers-Briggs Type Indicator (MBTI) (2001), Step II, Edmonton, AB: Consulting Psychologists Press.

International Spiritualist Review. (June 1960). A City that is set on a Hill Cannot be Hid. Vol. II, No. 1, Vancouver, Canada

Jaworski, J. (1998). Synchronicity: The Inner Path of Leadership. San Francisco: Berrett-Koehler Publishers.

Jung, C.G. (1959). The Basic Writings of C.G. Jung. In V.S. Laszlo (Ed.) New York: The Modern Library

Kaku, Michio (2012). The Universe in a Nutshell. Big Think http://www.youtube.com/watch?v=0NbBjNiw4tk

Kaku, Michio (2011). Explains String Theory. Floating University http://www.youtube.com/watch?v=0NbBjNiw4tk

Kirby, S. & McKenna, K. (1989). Experience, Research, Social Change: Methods from the Margins. Toronto, ON: Garamond Press

Kouzes, J.M. & Posner, B.Z. (1995). The Leadership Challenge. San Francisco: Jossey-Bass

Kuhn, Thomas, S. (1970). The Structure of Scientific Revolutions. Second Edition, Enlarged, Chicago: The University of Chicago Press

Marts, D. (March 2000). Intuitive Leadership: An Interview with James Wanless, Ph.D. Http://www.newtimes.org/issue/003/wanless.html.

MacKeracher, D. (1996). Making Sense of Adult Learning. Toronto, ON: Culture Concepts Inc.

Moore, L. (1992). Getting Past the Rapids: Voyageur Lessons Learned. Hamilton, ON: TranSkills

Myers, K. & Myers, P. (2002, June). Myers-Briggs Type Indicator—Step II. Victoria BC: Consulting Psychologist Press.

Nasmyth, G. (2003). Systematic Inquiry in Organizations. Course LT 513. Victoria, BC: Royal Roads University

Palmer, H. (Ed). (1998). Inner Knowing, Consciousness, Creativity and Insight. New York: Jeremy P. Tarcher.

Payls, T. (1997). Research Decisions, Quantitative and Qualitative Perspectives (2nd Ed). Scarborough, ON: Nelson, Thomson Canada Limited.

Pearce, J.D. (2011-2013) Spirit Science: Everything is connected. http://thespiritscience.net/spirit/about-spirit-science/

Quinn, R.E. (2000). Change the World: How Ordinary People Can Accomplish Extraordinary Results. San Francisco, CA: Jossey-Bass.

Richardson, L. (2000). Writing: A Method of Inquiry. (36) 923-948. Thousand Oaks, CA: Sage Publications.

Royal Roads University. (2003). Flow Chart for Courses in Master of Arts in Leadership and Training. School of Leadership (Available at Royal Roads University, 2005 Sooke Road, Victoria, BC V9B 5Y2)

Ruiz, D.M. (2004). The Voice of Knowledge: A Practical Guide to Inner Peace, San Rafael, California, Amber-Allen Publishing

Sams, J. & Carson, D. (1998). Medicine Cards: The Discovery of Power through the Ways of the Animals. Santa Fe, NM: Bear and Company

Schein, E.H. (1992). Organizational Culture and Leadership. San Francisco: Jossey-Bass

Schmidt, V.V. (1996). Awakening Intuition: A Delphi Study. Dissertation Abstracts, International Section A: The Humanities and Social Sciences

Secretan, L. (1997). Reclaiming Higher Ground: Creating Organizations that Inspire the Soul, Toronto, ON: MacMillan Canada

Sheldrake, R. & Fox, M. (1996). Natural Grace: Dialogues on Creation, Darkness and the Soul in Spirituality and Science. New York: Doubleday

Siegal, D.J., M.D. (2011). Mindsight: The New Science of Personal Transformation, New York, Bantam Books

Smith, M.K. (2001). Peter Senge and the Learning Organization. The Encyclopedia of Informal Education. www.infed.org/thinkers/senge.htm

Some, M.P. (1999). The Healing Wisdom of Africa: Finding Life Purpose through Nature, Ritual and Community. New York: Jeremy P. Tarcher/Putnam

Taylor, S. (1993 April). The Wisdom of Sprit. Essence, 23 (12), 57

Tieger, P. and Barron-Tieger, B. (1995). Do What You Are: Discover the Perfect Career for ou through the Secrets of Personality Type. Toronto: Little, Brown & Co.

Tolle, E. (2003). Stillness Speaks. Vancouver, BC: Namaste Publishing

Walsh, R. (1990). The Spirit of Shamanism. Los Angeles: Jeremy P. Tarcher

Watterson, M. (2013). Do You Know Who You Are? A Sacred Manual for Getting Spiritually Naked. N.Y: Hay House http://megganwatterson.com/

Weintraub, S. (1998). The Hidden Innovations through Intuition. Boston: Butterworth-Heinemann.

Wheatley, M.J. (1999). Leadership and the New Science: Discovering Order in a Chaotic World. San Francisco: Berrett-Koehler

Wolberg, T. (2003, March). Bright Lights. The Globe and Mail, pp. C1, C5